Bloom's

GUIDES

William Shakespeare's
Macbeth

CURRENTLY AVAILABLE

1984
All the Pretty Horses
Beloved
Brave New World
The Crucible
Cry, the Beloved Country
Death of a Salesman
Hamlet
The Handmaid's Tale
The House on Mango Street
I Know Why the Caged Bird Sings
Lord of the Flies
Macbeth
Maggie: A Girl of the Streets
Ragtime
The Scarlet Letter
Snow Falling on Cedars
To Kill a Mockingbird

Bloom's
GUIDES

William Shakespeare's
Macbeth

Edited & with an Introduction
by Harold Bloom

CHELSEA HOUSE
PUBLISHERS
A Haights Cross Communications Company
Philadelphia

A Haights Cross Communications Company

First Printing
1 3 5 7 9 8 6 4 2

Library of Congress Cataloging-in-Publication Data

Macbeth / edited and with an introduction by Harold Bloom.
     p. cm. — (Bloom's guides)
  Includes bibliographical references and index.
  ISBN 0-7910-7875-2
  1. Shakespeare, William, 1564-1616. Macbeth. 2. Macbeth, King of Scotland, 11th cent.—In literature. 3. Regicides in literature. I. Bloom, Harold. II. Series.
  PR2823.M2293 2004
  822.3'3—dc22
                                    2004001705

Chelsea House Publishers
1974 Sproul Road, Suite 400
Broomall, PA 19008-0914

www.chelseahouse.com

Contributing editor: Janyce Marson
Cover design by Takeshi Takahashi
Layout by EJB Publishing Services

Contents

Introduction

HAROLD BLOOM

Macbeth ought to be the least sympathetic of Shakespeare's hero-villains. He is a murderer of old men, women, and children, and has a particular obsession with overcoming time by murdering the future: hence his failed attempt to kill Fleance, and his successful slaughter of Macduff's children. And yet the playgoer and the reader cannot resist identifying with the imagination of Macbeth. A great killing-machine, Macbeth has few attributes beyond imagination to recommend him, and that imagination itself is anything but benign. Yet it is open to the powers of the air and of the night: occult, mediumlike, prophetic, and moral at least in part, it must be the most singular imagination in all of Shakespeare's plays. And yet it has great limitations; it is not much allied to Macbeth's far more ordinary, indeed inadequate intellectual powers. Its autonomy, together with its desperate strength, is what destroys all of Macbeth's victims, and at last Macbeth himself. Imagination or "fantasy" is an equivocal term in the Renaissance, where it can mean both poetic furor, a personal replacement for divine inspiration, and a loss-in-reality, perhaps as a consequence of such a displacement of sacred by secular.

Shakespeare has no single position in regard to the fantasy-making power, whether in *Macbeth* or in *A Midsummer Night's Dream* or *The Tempest*. Yet all these are visionary dramas, and in some sense pragmatically exalt imagination even as they question it. But *Macbeth* is a tragedy, and a visionary tragedy is a strange genre. Like Hamlet, Othello, and Lear, Macbeth is a tragic protagonist, and yet like Claudius, Iago, and Edmund, Macbeth is a villain, indeed a monster of murderousness far surpassing the others. We find it difficult, as we read or watch a performance of *Macbeth*, to think of its protagonist as a criminal dictator, a small-scale Hitler or Stalin, and yet he is pragmatically just that. I do not think that Macbeth's wistful scruples, his nostalgias and regrets, draw us to him; he is never in any danger of collapsing back into the innocence he rarely ceases to crave. The reader and playgoer needs to ask: "Why, even in despite of myself, do I identify with Macbeth, down to the very end?" It cannot be that Macbeth's desires and ambitions essentially are our own; even if the Oedipal desire to slay the father (the good King Duncan) is universal. Even if we are all would-be usurpers, most of us presumably do not desire to terrorize our societies. The appeal of Macbeth, hardly to be resisted, seems to me at the heart of Shakespeare's concerns in this great domestic tragedy of blood.

Macbeth's imagination is at once his greatest strength and his destructive weakness, yet it does not provoke an ambivalence in us. We thrill to its poetic, expressionistic strength, whatever its consequences. Shakespeare, on some level, may be making a critique of his own imagination, which has much in common with Macbeth's, and yet the play is anything but a condemnation of the Macbethian imagination. Indeed, as Macbeth increasingly becomes outraged by the equivocal nature of the occult promises that have been made to him, his sense of being outraged contaminates us, so that we come to share in his outrage. He becomes our paradigm of confounded expectations, and we are moved by him as we are moved by Captain Ahab, who in Melville's *Moby-Dick* plays the role of an American Macbeth. Ahab is not a murderer, and yet his obsessive hunt for *Moby-Dick* destroys the *Pequod* and its entire crew, except for the storytelling Ishmael. Melville modeled Ahab's imagination upon Macbeth's, and a close comparison of Ahab and Macbeth is capable of illuminating both figures. Like Ahab, Macbeth is made into a monomaniac by his compulsive imagination, though killing King Duncan has little in common with the vain attempt to kill the White Whale, who has maimed poor Ahab. Still, like Ahab, Macbeth attempts to strike through the mask of natural appearances in order to uncover the malign principles that, at least in part, would seem to govern the universe. The cosmos, both in Shakespeare's play and in Melville's prose-epic, seems to have resulted from a creation that was also a fall. Both Macbeth and Ahab are central and appropriate to their universes; their imaginings of disaster bring about fresh disasters, and their battles against their own sense of having been outraged by supernatural forces bring about cataclysmic disorders, both for themselves and nearly everyone else about them.

The comparison between Macbeth and his descendant Ahab has its limits. Ahab's guilt is only that of an instrument; he leads his crew to destruction, but he himself is neither a tyrant nor a usurper. Macbeth, a far greater figure than Shakespeare's Richard III or his Claudius, nevertheless is in their tradition: he is a plotter and an assassin. And yet he has sublimity; an authentic tragic grandeur touches and transfigures him. That difference arises again from the nature and power of his prophetic imagination, which is far too strong for every other faculty in him to battle. Macbeth's mind, character, affections are all helpless when confronted by the strength and prevalence of his fantasy, which does his thinking, judging, and feeling for him. Before he scarcely is conscious of a desire, wish, or ambition, the image of the accomplished deed already dominates him, long before the act is performed. Macbeth sees, sometimes quite literally, the phantasmagoria of the future. He is an involuntary visionary, and there is something baffling about his ambition to become king. What do he and Lady Macbeth wish to do with their royal status and power, once they have it? An evening with King and Queen Macbeth at court is an affair apocalyptically dismal: the frightened Thanes brood as to just who will be murdered next, and the graciousness of their hostess seems adequately represented by her famous dismissal to stay not upon the order of their going, but go! Whether the Macbeths still hope for progeny is ambiguous, as is the question of whether they have had children who then died, but they seem to share a dread of futurity. Macbeth's horror of time, often remarked by his critics, has a crucial relation to his uncanniest aspect, transcending fantasy, because he seems to sense a realm free of time yet at least as much a nightmare as his time-obsessed existence. Something in Macbeth really is most at home in the world of the witches and of Hecate. Against the positive transcendence of Hamlet's charismatic personality, Shakespeare set the negative transcendence of Macbeth's hag-ridden nature. And yet a negative transcendence remains a transcendence; there are no flights of angels to herald the end of Macbeth, but there is the occult breakthrough that persuades us, at last, that the time is free.

Biographical Sketch

Few events in the life of William Shakespeare are supported by reliable evidence, and many incidents recorded by commentators of the last four centuries are either conjectural or apocryphal.

William Shakespeare was born in Stratford-upon-Avon on April 22 or 23, 1564, the son of Mary Arden and John Shakespeare, a tradesman. His early education was in the hands of a tutor, for his parents were probably illiterate. At age seven he entered the Free School in Stratford, where he learned the "small Latin and less Greek" attributed to him by Ben Jonson. When not in school Shakespeare may have gone to the popular Stratford fairs and to the dramas and mystery plays performed by traveling actors.

When Shakespeare was about thirteen his father removed him from school and apprenticed him to a butcher, although it is not known how long he remained in this occupation. When he was eighteen he married Anne Hathaway; their first child, Susanna, was born six months later. Twins Hamnet and Judith were born in February 1585. About this time Shakespeare was caught poaching deer on the estate of Sir Thomas Lucy of Cherlecot; Lucy's prosecution is said to have inspired Shakespeare to write his earliest literary work, a satire on his opponent. Shakespeare was convicted of poaching and forced to leave Stratford. He withdrew to London, leaving his family behind. He soon attached himself to the stage, initially in a menial capacity (as tender of playgoers' horses, according to one tradition), then as prompter's attendant. When the poaching furor subsided, Shakespeare returned to Stratford to join one of the many bands of itinerant actors. In the next five years he gained what little theatre training he received.

By 1592 Shakespeare was a recognized actor, and in that year he wrote and produced his first play, *Henry the Sixth, Part One*. Its success impelled Shakespeare soon afterward to write the second and third parts of *Henry the Sixth*. Shakespeare's popularity provoked the jealousy of Robert Greene, as recorded in his posthumous *Groats-worth of Wit* (1592). Shakespeare published *Venus and Adonis* in 1593, a poem based upon Ovid (or perhaps upon Arthur Golding's translation of Ovid's *Metamorphoses*). It was dedicated to the young Earl of Southampton—but perhaps without permission, a possible indication that Shakespeare was trying to gain the nobleman's patronage. However, the dedicatory address to Southampton in the poem *The Rape of Lucrece* (1594) reveals Shakespeare to have been on good terms with him. Many plays—such as *Titus Andronicus*, *The Comedy of Errors*, and *Romeo and Juliet*—were produced over the next several years, most performed by Shakespeare's troupe, the Lord Chamberlain's Company. In December 1594 Shakespeare acted in a comedy (of unknown authorship) before Queen Elizabeth; many other royal performances followed in the next decade.

In August 1596 Shakespeare's son Hamnet died. Early the next year Shakespeare bought a home, New Place, in the center of Stratford; he is said to have planted a mulberry tree in the back yard with his own hands. Shakespeare's relative prosperity is indicated by his purchasing more than a hundred acres of farmland in 1602, a cottage near his estate later that year, and half-interest in the tithes of some local villages in 1605.

In September 1598 Shakespeare began his friendship with the then unknown Ben Jonson by producing his play *Every Man in His Humour*. The next year the publisher William Jaggard affixed Shakespeare's name, without his permission, to a curious medley of poems under the title *The Passionate Pilgrim*; the majority of the poems were not by Shakespeare. Two of his sonnets, however, appeared in this collection, although the 154 sonnets, with their mysterious dedication to "Mr. W. H.," were not published as a group until 1609. Also in 1599 the Globe Theatre was built in Southwark (an area of London), and Shakespeare's company began acting there. Many of his greatest plays—*Troilus and Cressida*, *King Lear*, *Othello*, *Macbeth*—were performed in the Globe before its destruction by fire in 1613.

The death in 1603 of Queen Elizabeth, the last of the Tudors, and the accession of James I, from the Stuart dynasty of Scotland, created anxiety throughout England. Shakespeare's fortunes, however, were unaffected, as the new monarch extended the license of Shakespeare's company to perform at the Globe. James I saw a performance of Othello at the court in November 1604. In October 1605 Shakespeare's company performed before the Mayor and Corporation of Oxford. The last five years of Shakespeare's life seem void of incident; he had retired from the stage by 1613. Among the few known incidents is Shakespeare's involvement in a heated and lengthy dispute about the enclosure of common-fields around Stratford. He died on April 23, 1616, and was buried in the Church of St. Mary's in Stratford. A monument was later erected to him in the Poets' Corner of Westminster Abbey.

The Story Behind the Story

Hospitality in *Macbeth*

Many critics have commented on the status of hospitality in *Macbeth* and the numerous ways in which the obligations incumbent upon host and hostess are subverted in this very dark and violent tragedy. Though the history of hospitality is vast and infinitely varied, what follows is, by necessity, a very brief and simplified overview of the historical, spiritual, and social dimensions of hospitality that are relevant to an understanding of *Macbeth* and the time in which it was written.

Hospitality, from the Latin *hospitalias*, refers to the practice of receiving and entertaining guests with generosity and goodwill, as well as the provision of food and safe lodging. It is an extremely important concept encompassing ethical, political, and religious duties inherited from classical and medieval interpretations and, most importantly for *Macbeth*, early 17th century interpretations of the social obligations incumbent upon King and court during state functions. Indeed, so important is the notion of hospitality as a means of political and communal stability and civic life that it is codified from its earliest time.

As Seneca has been identified as an influence for Shakespeare and his contemporaries, and for *Macbeth* in particular, the Senecan perspective on hospitality is relevant. A philosopher of the Stoic school of ancient Rome (4 BC–65 AD), Seneca was interested in the fulfillment of an individual's ethical obligations. In *De Beneficiss*, Seneca emphasizes the role of the giver of hospitality over the object given or the reaction of the recipient. "External actions were not irrelevant, but were treated as instrumental means of to the achievement of inner virtue or peace of mind."[1]. When we apply this definition of a balanced and orderly existence to *Macbeth*, we immediately understand how utterly devoid of virtue and well-being is life both in the court and in the psychological state of its host and hostess. Indeed, *Macbeth* and his queen are so consumed with greed that they are utterly incapable of manifesting anything but self-serving gestures and bloody deeds in their relentless pursuit of power.

For a variety of reasons, *Macbeth* has also been characterized as a medieval play and, thus, the monastic tradition that evolved during the long history of the Middle Ages is likewise relevant. The most important manifestation of a code of hospitality is found in the religious orders, such as the Rule of St. Benedict, wherein an adherence to the tenets of hospitality is crucial to the formation of Christian character both within the religious community and to society in general. "The Benedictine Rule required that monasteries welcome all travelers, though pilgrims and believers were singled out as deserving particular welcome... Nevertheless, in both cases, it is the host who guarantees the safety and comfort of the lodger and, in so doing, integrates the lodger into the larger group."[2] Furthermore, hospitality was considered part of Christian charity and an important way of fulfilling one's obligation to perform good works. Finally, within the medieval monastic tradition we can identify a quasi-political agenda, not very different from classical notions, insofar as hospitality and ethical responsibility are seen as necessary for the maintenance of law and order both within the monastery and the larger community without, albeit framed within a spiritual context. As to the issue of good governance, the world over which Macbeth presides is a chaotic one from which both royal and aristocratic guests must flee in order to save their lives, a realm from which there can be no safe haven or hospitable reception for guests or visitors.

Finally, in the context of the time in which *Macbeth* was written, the early 17th century reign of King James I, hospitality acquires a more secular and politically-motivated agenda, though the paradigms of both classical ethics and Christian values remain the guiding principles. For royalty and aristocracy the rules of hospitality become the means for regulating a healthy body politic and preserving the status quo for the privileged class. More specifically, as proof of just how compelling this need to preserve class distinction really was, a series of proclamations, issued from the 1590's to the later 1630s, during the reign of Elizabeth, James, and Charles, forbade the gentry to live in or about the city outside the law terms, and mandated their return to the country to stabilize rural relationships during times of harvest failure, thereby preventing the traditional seat of social protocol from being lost due to an absentee nobility.[3] With respect to the rules of hospitality in the banquet hall, this dual aspect of public and private interests is again demonstrated.

> the tradition of the banquet, in Renaissance tragedy, evokes the split between private political aims and public duties of care. at the same time, it demonstrates the source of a ruler's vulnerability in the gap between hospitable strategies and tactics....[4]

From this particular perspective, Macbeth provides numerous examples of a subversive practice of hospitality at the royal household at Dunsinane: the guests are in mortal danger once they enter the gates of the castle; the host and hostess are so preoccupied that, at the very least, they neglect their obligation to entertain their guests, and at the very worst, they display an unseemly loss of emotional control for all to see; the very nature of the banquet is transformed from a celebration of good food and fellowship into a living nightmare where guests are poisoned and murdered in their chambers; and the aristocratic society in attendance must leave with great haste, abandoning all rules of protocol and social privilege.

Finally, in addition to the stage providing a forum for representing contemporary notions of hospitality, a wide range of writers, including pamphleteers, preachers, poets and historians, were also defining the practice of hospitality. The period of 1580 to 1630 saw an abundance of pamphlets which chronicled both the diminution of the rules of hospitality from ancient and medieval notions of the rules of propriety. "Drawing sustenance from classical authors such as Martial and Juvenal and from Old and New Testament sources, these publications anatomized contemporary culture in moral, economic, and religious terms. In ways unavailable to the theater, pamphleteers claimed for their representations the status of reportage, of a simple presentation of the manifold versions of hospitable practice, its successes and failures."[5] On April 29, 1604, while moving from feast to feast on his way back to London, James I made several stops along the way to collect gifts of gold, prize horses, falcons and poetry, an event that became memorialized in a pamphlet entitled The True Narration of the Entertainment of His Royal Majesty, combining social commentary with reportage.[6] These royal "progressions" would become codified through custom.

Recently, another paradigm for the status of hospitality in Macbeth is offered in which Macbeth's tragedy is characterized as a self-imposed exile from home. Through his insistence upon living in the future, Macbeth can neither live in the present nor be present to himself. "The most unnerving form of exile, then, must be exile in the home—when that which should be the safest, most intimate, the most at-an-end becomes alien and restless. Such an uncanny exile is a common feature of tragedy and of tragic figures, but none more so than Macbeth."[7] For the bloody deeds Macbeth must commit to secure the throne, he is condemned to remain an unlawful king, consumed by a misguided faith in false prophesies and the evil agents who deliver them. Living in a state of self-imposed exile, Macbeth is rendered utterly incapable of extending a gracious and hospitable welcome to anyone else.

Notes

1. Heal, Felicity. *Hospitality in Modern England*. Oxford and New York: Oxford University Press (1990): 101.

2. Cowell, Andrew. At Play in the tavern: Signs, Coins, and bodies in the Middle Ages. Ann Arbor: The University of Michigan Press, 1999.

3. Heal, 118.

4. Palmer, Daryl W. *Hospitable Performances: Dramatic Genre and Cultural Practices in Early Modern England*. West Lafayette, Indiana: Purdue University Press (1992): Cambridge and New York: Cambridge University Press (2000): 175.

5. Palmer., 34.

6. Palmer., 121.

7. Burnham, Douglas. "Language, Time and Politics in Shakespeare's *Macbeth*." From *Displaced Persons: Conditions of Exile in European Culture*. Edited by Sharon Ouditt. Burlington, VT: Ashgate Publishing Company (2002): 28.

List of Characters

At the start of the play, **Macbeth** is a military hero whose misguided ambition leads him to murder King Duncan and usurp the throne of Scotland, as well as to commit other evil acts. His crimes cause him to sink into a state of psychological turmoil, as rebel forces lead an attack against him.

Lady Macbeth is the wife of Macbeth, who is even more driven by greed and power than her husband, and is the manipulative force behind the murder of Duncan. Like her husband, she becomes tortured by her bloody deeds, goes mad and kills herself.

Duncan is the King of Scotland who is murdered by Macbeth. His death causes the country to descend into chaos.

Malcolm, King Duncan's oldest son, is the rightful heir to the throne of Scotland who flees to England after his father's murder and later returns to lead a successful attack against Macbeth.

Banquo is a general in Duncan's army and a close friend of Macbeth prior to Macbeth's seizing the throne. When Macbeth begins to fear Banquo's former allegiance to King Duncan and his son's future claim to the throne, he has him murdered.

Fleance is Banquo's son and heir. Although Macbeth attempts to murder him with his father, Fleance's survival ensures that Banquo's line will persist to fulfill the witches' prophecy.

Macduff is a general in Duncan's army who becomes suspicious of Macbeth's part in Duncan's murder. He flees to England to enlist Malcolm's help in fighting Macbeth and encourage him to seize his rightful crown. While Macduff is in England, Macbeth murders his entire family. Macduff vows personal revenge against the tyrant and succeeds in beheading him during battle.

The Three Witches are the personification of evil who prophesy that Macbeth will become the King of Scotland, planting the seed of greed in his mind with their enigmatic predictions. Tragically, Macbeth does not understand that he is being fed with riddles.

Donalbain is Duncan's youngest son who flees to Ireland after his father's murder and does not return.

Lennox is one of Duncan's nobles who accompanies Macbeth to Duncan's chambers after his murder. Lenox is suspicious of Macbeth and fearful for Scotland.

Ross is a Scottish noble and cousin to Macduff. He brings the good news of Macbeth's military victory but also the bad news about Macduff's murdered family.

Siward is the Earl of Northumberland and veteran military officer. He later becomes an ally of Malcolm and Macduff and leads the first attack against Macbeth's forces.

Young Siward is the son of Siward who follows his father to fight against Macbeth in Scotland; he is killed in a duel with Macbeth.

Seton is the only remaining officer in Macbeth's army that remains loyal to him.

Hecate is the queen of the witches.

Summary and Analysis

Macbeth is a tragic play about a heroic warrior who falls from grace when he allows himself to be seduced by the promise of boundless power, a man duped by false prophesies delivered by the forces of evil, and an unlawful king whose reign is as temporary as it is violent and unstable. Riddled with ambivalence, and himself the victim of the prophesies of the three witches, or the Weird Sisters, Macbeth steals the throne of Scotland from the rightful successor, Prince Malcolm, by murdering King Duncan. In so doing, Macbeth brings nothing but chaos to his realm as evil begets further evil and, ultimately, becomes the agent of his own demise. A brave warrior returning victorious from a great battle, Macbeth is praised and rewarded by King Duncan of Scotland, who bestows the title and privileges of a thane upon him. However, after his encounter with the Weird Sisters and their prediction of his future kingship, Macbeth's character begins to deteriorate rapidly. Placing his trust in the wrong "advisors" and adhering to a blind faith in false deities, he is driven to bloody and criminal acts by an overwhelming sense of greed and desire for power. He also has a wife who is even more obsessed with becoming Queen, one who manipulates her husband by attacking his masculinity when he displays an appropriate response to his murderous deeds, and glibly dismisses all evidence that could assign culpability. Nevertheless, Macbeth remains a character whom it is difficult to completely define. Consumed by guilt and apprehension, he still retains a small portion of his former heroic valor as he prays for a newly-restored and healthy Scotland just moments before his death.

ACT I

From the very brief opening scene, the audience enters a dark and foreboding landscape, a desolate heath, inhabited by three witches who have gathered into an open field during a dark thunderstorm. They agree that at their next gathering they will meet with Macbeth, "[w]hen the hurlyburly's done," implying that they will play games with his character, enticing him to evil. Their final cackling statement that "[f]air is foul, and foul is fair," foreshadows one of the central themes of the play, namely how to interpret contrary signs and enigmatic statements, how to distinguish between appearance and reality. And their sense of urgency in meeting with Macbeth "ere the set of sun," introduces the issue of the type of temporality that exists throughout the play, namely an impatience with the present that causes Macbeth (and others) to get ahead of himself in his desire to manifest predictions of future political gain. In the following short scene (**scene 2**), we are in King Duncan's camp, where an unnamed captain, bleeding from battle wounds, praises Macbeth's bravery, "[l]ike Valour's minion," in his battle with Macdonwald. Nevertheless, as soon as this victory is accomplished, Sweno, the Norwegian King, sees his enemy's vulnerability as they celebrate and launches a fresh assault upon Macbeth, and is defeated once again. Shortly after the captain departs to tend his wounds, the Thane of Rosse appears and informs Duncan that the Thane of Cawdor became a traitor, having joined forces with the King of Norway. Enraged by this last report, Duncan resolves to kill this traitor and bestows the title upon Macbeth, making him the new Thane of Cawdor.

Scene 3 returns us to the three witches on a dismal heath, with one of them promising to avenge an insult from a sailor's wife by sending tempestuous winds to bandy about her husband's boat and deprive him of sleep, while the others offer their assistance with this diabolical plot. As they brew their magic potion, the three weird sisters join hands and dance around nine times. In the meantime, a drum roll is heard as Macbeth and Banquo enter. Unbeknownst to him, Macbeth ironically repeats the words of the three witches in the very first scene as he comments on the foul weather on the heath. "So foul and fair a day I have not seen." But it is Banquo who first describes the witches as fantastic creatures, bearing no resemblance to "inhabitants of the earth," as he describes their horrible skinny lips, chappy fingers, and beards, which features make them appear like men though they are not so. When

Macbeth questions them, the witches respond by hailing him three times and greeting him as something he has not yet become—the Thane of Cawdor and the future king. Macbeth is completely baffled by the witches' riddle, "[t]hou shalt get kings, though thou be none," while Banquo begs to hear about his own future. The witches response to Banquo is equally incomprehensible, that he will be "lesser than Macbeth and greater" and "not so happy, yet much happier." They also foretell that he shall beget kings. But when Macbeth begs to hear more, to know why and how these "imperfect speakers" are able to make their predictions, the three weird creatures quickly vanish without answering, and the men are left to puzzle over their strange encounter, questioning whether their observations are credible or the result of having eaten of some "insane root."

However, they are soon interrupted by the arrival of Ross and Angus, the Scottish noblemen sent by King Duncan. The two messengers tell of the king's appreciation for Macbeth's bravery and victory and reveal that he has been granted the title of Thane of Cawdor—just as the witches had predicted. Shocked by the realization of the witches' prediction, Banquo questions whether the devil, in the form of these three witches, can speak the truth, while Macbeth wonders how two men can bear the same title. Angus then explains that Cawdor is to be executed for treasonous acts. Though Macbeth is overjoyed with his seeming good luck, he nevertheless has grave doubts about the unfolding events and the eventuality that he will be king by murdering Duncan. "Present fears / Are less than horrible imaginings. / My thought, whose murther yet is fantastical, / Shakes so my single state of man." And, as Banquo has just warned him, evil only speaks half truths, "win us with honest trifles," only to deceive by making appearances seem like reality. The seeds of greed having been firmly planted, Macbeth leaves off his musing about the mixed message by declaring that "[n]othing is but what is not." which succinctly summarizes the appearance versus reality theme. The scene ends with Macbeth leaving the future to Chance.

Scene 4 takes place at King Duncan's palace at Forres, the king having arrived with his sons, Malcolm and Donalbain, along with Lennox and other attendants. Malcolm informs Duncan that the former Thane of Cawdor has been executed. Ironically, Duncan responds that it is easy to read someone's character by their physiognimy. "There's no art / To find the mind's construction in the face." When Macbeth and Banquo arrive with Ross and Angus, Duncan greets the new Thane of Cawdor as "worthiest cousin," thanking both him and Banquo for their loyal service. He tells Macbeth, "I have begun to plant thee, and will labour / To make thee full of growing," but promises to reward Banquo in a similar manner, and names Malcolm as Prince of Cumberland and the heir to the throne. Macbeth is disturbed by this last pronouncement and, in an aside, hopes that the stars will no allow the "light to see my black and deep desires." The scene concludes with Duncan announcing that he will visit Macbeth at Inverness, thus providing Macbeth with the opportunity to murder him.

Scene 5 begins with Lady Macbeth reading a letter from her husband, informing her of the royal visit and his previous encounter with the three witches and their predictions of his future political gain. Elated by the prospect of becoming queen, ambitious and ruthless Lady Macbeth is anxious about her husband's perceived weakness and inability to carry out any plan that would insure his success. Thus, she looks forward to his speedy return and decides to take control of their shared destiny. "Hie thee hither, / That I may pour my spirits in thine ear." When an attendant informs her of Duncan's arrival, she welcomes his "fatal entrance" and begs the spirits to assist her in her deadly plan by removing all vestiges of feminine weakness. "Unsex me here, / And fill me, from the crown to the toe, top-full / Of direst cruelty!" When Macbeth enters the scene, she makes her first proleptic gesture by greeting him as a king, calling him the "all hail hereafter" and immediately proceeds to share her murderous plot against Duncan with him. "I feel now the future is in the instant." She also warns Macbeth not to let this diabolical plot to show in his face. "Your face, my Thane, is as a book, where men / May read strange matters." Macbeth approves and the scene closes with Lady Macbeth telling him to remain calm and "leave the rest to me."

Scene 6 is brief and opens outside Inverness Castle where King Duncan has arrived with his sons, Banquo, and other noblemen and attendants. Both Duncan and Banquo admire the castle, believing the "temple-haunting marlet" to be heaven sent and a harbinger of good omens. As they discuss the merits of Inverness, the duplicitous Lady Macbeth, who has all along been plotting Duncan's murder, comes out to greet them, appearing to be the perfect hostess whose sole concern is to serve her guests. "We rest your hermits."

Scene 7 opens with the solitary Macbeth wrestling with his conscience and his plot to murder his benevolent king and guest at a time when he is required to play the proper host. A brief psychomachia seems to be suggested here, wherein the conflict between good and evil rages in his soul. Nevertheless, Macbeth's conscience gives way to political expediency as he makes the necessary leap against all ethical considerations. "I have no spur / To prick the sides of my intent, but only / Vaulting ambition, which o'erleaps itself / And falls on th'other–." Aware of Macbeth's ambivalence, his wife unmercifully attacks his masculinity, calling him a fearful coward. Though he protests this cruel accusation, Lady Macbeth issues a fresh tirade against him and laughs at his anxiety that their plot may fail. She plans to pin the murder on Duncan's two guards, getting them intoxicated and then smearing them with the king's blood while the sleep away their stupor. Against his better judgment, Macbeth acquiesces to the plan.

ACT II

Scene 1 opens at Inverness around midnight with Banquo and his son Fleance having a conversation before retiring to bed. Banquo observes the foreboding darkness of a starless sky. He is afraid to fall asleep lest he have bad dreams of the three wicked witches. However, when Macbeth enters the scene, Banquo's first response is to praise both him and Lady Macbeth for their hospitality. Macbeth also learns that the king has gone happily to his bed for the night. When Banquo finally tells Macbeth about his dreams of the three weird sisters, Macbeth replies, hypocritically, "he does not think of them."

Nevertheless, despite his praise for his host, when Macbeth asks for Banquo's loyalty should he become king, the latter promises on the condition that his kingship be honorable and free from evil. After Banquo and Fleance depart for bed, Macbeth is left by himself to face his fears and envisions a dagger in front of him. But when Macbeth attempts to seize it, nothing is there. Though he blinks his eyes to erase the image, the dagger remains and is now dripping blood. Macbeth finally understands that it is only a vision of the "bloody business at hand" while his thoughts turn to the witching hour of midnight when "witchcraft celebrates." The scene ends with the sounding of a bell, ringing Duncan's death knell. Macbeth leaves as there is no more time for procrastination.

Lady Macbeth enters in **scene 2,** declaring aloud that the wine which "made them drunk hath made me bold." She has left the daggers out for Macbeth to use and says that if the king had not resembled her own father in his sleep, she probably would have killed him herself. Macbeth has done the dastardly deed himself and returns, visibly shaken, covered in blood and carrying the two murder weapons. "Methought, I heard a voice cry, 'Sleep no more! / Macbeth does murther Sleep.'" In a play in which insomnia becomes a curse, Macbeth believes that he has heard a voice crying to him that "[s]leep no more, Macbeth does murder sleep." For her part, Lady Macbeth interrupts his horrifying thoughts with calculated and practical detachment, warning him to wash away the evidence and return the daggers to the crime scene. But the tormented Macbeth responds that he will go no more. "I am afraid to think what I have done; / Look on it again I dare not." Resigned to do it herself, Lady Macbeth departs as Macbeth hears a loud and repetitious knocking that causes him to panic. True to her character, Lady Macbeth criticizes his cowardly anxiety and then admonishes him not to be lost "so poorly in your thoughts." But Macbeth's guilt and anxiety have already taken root. "To know my deed, twere best not know myself."

In **scene 3** the knocking that began in the prior scene intensifies until one of the drunken porters awakens and comes to the door of the castle. The porter imagines himself opening hell's gate where a number of sinners are waiting to come in, including a greedy farmer who hanged himself, an equivocator who "committed treason enough for God's sake," and an English tailor who was a thief. It is no coincidence that each one of these sinners possesses one of Macbeth's tragic flaws: The farmer is greedy; the equivocator is full of pretense and lies; and the tailor is a thief, like Macbeth who has just stolen Duncan's life. When the porter actually opens the door, it is Macduff and Lennox who have come to wake the king. In a very humorous and witty interlude, the porter talks to the two of them about the enervating effects of alcohol, until Macbeth appears, offering to lead them to Duncan's room. While Macduff enters the king's chambers, Lennox tells Macbeth the frightening details of a storm and earthquake that had taken place during the night, in which strange screams of death were heard. Such happenings were considered to be prophesies of "dire combustion and confused events" (a political reference to the chaotic, war-torn status of Scotland). Their conversation, however, is soon interrupted by the wild-eyed Macduff screaming of the king's murder. "Confusion hath made his masterpiece! / Most sacrilegious Murther has broke ope / The Lord's anointed Temple, and stole thence / The life o' th' building." In the midst of this scene of chaos, Lady Macbeth enters calmly and inquires about what is going on.

When Macbeth and Lennox return, Macbeth makes an eloquent attempt to express his grief, which is hypocritical given his direct culpability yet truthful in its analysis of the bloody deeds that have transpired. "I had liv'd a blessed time; for, from this instant, / There's nothing serious in mortality; / All is but toys; renown, and grace, is dead." As he concludes this speech, the king's sons, Malcolm and Donalbain, enter and learn of their father's death, while Macbeth confesses to having killed both servants out of feigned fury for a crime they did not commit. Lady Macbeth pretends to have fainted as another diversionary tactic. Banquo closes the scene by requesting a meeting while Malcolm and Donalbain go their separate ways to England and Ireland, in order to protect themselves from the murderer.

Scene 4 opens the next morning outside Macbeth's castle with Ross and an old man conversing about the tragedy that occurred in the last scene. Stating that in his seventy years he has never known such dreadful times, Ross adds that heaven is showing its displeasure with mankind, for though it is morning, "darkness does the face of earth entomb, when living light should kiss it." As this conversation continues, Macduff enters and says that he too is in a dark and dismal mood wanting to hear further news about the murder. Though Macduff reports that Malcolm and Donalbain are suspected of foul play, Ross quickly remarks that it is highly unnatural for a son to kill his father. A wary Macduff then reveals that Macbeth has been chosen king and is already at Scone for his coronation, while Duncan's body has been taken to Colmekill, "the sacred storehouse of this predecessors," to be buried. Macduff is going home to Fife, but Ross plans to go to Scone for the coronation. Macduff departs and the scene closes with a blessing from the old man.

ACT III

Scene 1 opens at the palace at Forres with Banquo alone and speaking aloud to an absent and highly suspect Macbeth, the newly crowned King. "Thou hast it now, King, Cawdor, Glamis, all, as the weird women promised, and I fear thou play'dst most foully for't." Banquo's thoughts about the witches' prediction for him are interrupted by the sound of a trumpet as King Macbeth and the Queen enter with Lennox, Ross and other lords, ladies, and attendants. The king invites Banquo to the banquet he is holding in the evening and then asks Banquo a series of questions to find out what his plans are for the rest of the day and with whom. After he has sent Banquo off for his afternoon ride and the others have left to enjoy themselves, Macbeth delivers a soliloquy in which he states that to be king is nothing unless the king is safe. He does not feel safe for Banquo, "hath a wisdom that doth guide his valour to act in safety ... and under him, my genius is rebuked." He also reveals his jealous fears that Banquo's sons will some day be kings instead of his future offspring. "Upon my head they plac'd a fruitless crown, / And put a barren sceptre in my gripe, / Thence to be wrench't with an unlineal hand, /No son of mine succeeding." By the end of the soliloquy, Macbeth indicates that he has no other choice than to kill both Banquo and his son Fleance. In furtherance of his evil ways, when a servant enters with the two common murderers that Macbeth has sent for, Macbeth fabricates a persuasive story to convince the two of them that Banquo has treated them poorly. "Are you so gospell'd, / To pray for this good man, and for his issue, Whose heavy hand hath bow'd you to the grave, / And beggar'd yours forever." Macbeth's manipulation ends in his asking them to murder Banquo and Fleance, while exercising extreme caution lest they be discovered. The murder is to take place on this very night away from the palace and the scene concludes with Macbeth addressing an absent Banquo. "It is concluded: Banquo, thy soul's flight, / If it find Heaven, must find it out to-night."

Scene 2 opens with Lady Macbeth sending a servant to fetch the king. While awaiting the king's arrival, she shows her concern for the brooding and fearful Macbeth. "Tis safer to be that which we destroy than by destruction dwell in doubtful joy." Still the cool and calculating pragmatist, she questions Macbeth on why had persists in highly anxious state. "Why do you keep alone of sorriest fancies your companions making? ... What's done is done." Macbeth's response is that they have only succeeded in wounding the snake, not killing it. For his part, Macbeth's fear of retribution for his murderous acts are growing, so much so that he state he would rather be dead than to endure the "torture of mind" with which he must live. Surprisingly, Lady Macbeth acts outside her character by not criticizing his fears and, instead, resorting to a gentle warns of the need to appear happy before his dinner guests. Macbeth promises to disguise his innermost thoughts and asks her to pay special attention to Banquo during the meal. So perturbed is Macbeth that he seems to have forgotten his plan to murder Banquo before dinner. She tells him to quit worrying about Banquo and Fleance, but the audience, like Macbeth, knows this is an impossibility. In fact, the king replies to his wife that his mind is "full of scorpions" and that "there shall be done a deed of dreadful note." When Lady Macbeth asks what is to be done, her husband leaves her in the dark, saying to her, "Be innocent of the knowledge till thou applaud the deed." He is in complete charge now as he was not previously. Still confident that Lady Macbeth will agree with the murders after they are accomplished, the scene ends with Macbeth once again asking for night to come quickly, now in order "cancel and tear to pieces that great bond (Banquo) which keeps me paled." But Macbeth is a frightfully haunted man, determined to kill Fleance and living in fear of being discovered throughout the day, and of a darkness which offers no relief since he is plagued by terrible dreams.

Scene 3 takes place in a park outside the palace where the two original murderers are joined by a third, sent by Macbeth. As the scene opens, the three of them are waiting for Banquo and Fleance to return from their ride in the countryside in order to carry out their murderous deed. Banquo and Fleance, entering the park, are depicted as two medieval travellers approaching an inn at the end of a day to find safe lodging for the night. As they approach, the murderers set upon them, stabbing Banquo first. Banquo, knowing that he is about to die, screams out to Fleance directing him to flee the palace. "Fly, good Fleance, fly, fly, fly! / Thou may'st revenge—O slave!" Though Banquo dies, his son escapes on foot into the darkness of the night, while the murderers express regret that Fleance's escape leaves their job woefully incomplete in that they have not eliminated Macbeth's contender for the throne.

Scene 4, which takes place in the banquet hall, opens with Macbeth's entrance accompanied by his queen and his lords and attendants, and is an important scene in that it is consumed with flashbacks, symbolism, imagery, and irony. At first the banquet scene presents a confident Macbeth, assuming his obligation as "the humble host," welcoming the guests, and the hall a picture of perfect order. "[H]ere I'll sit i' th' midst. / Be large in mirth; anon, we'll drink a measure / The table round." Macbeth, indeed, seems a man in perfect control, able to conceal his innermost disturbed thoughts, while greeting his guests. But this guise of self-control, quickly becomes undone as he comes face to face with the first murderer. Noting that the murderer has blood on his face, he is informed that the blood belongs to Banquo. Paling at the news that Fleance has escaped with his life, Macbeth begins to unravel. "Then comes my fit again, ... / I am cabin'd, cribb'd, confin'd, bound in / To saucy doubts and fears." And this expression of anxiety serves to foreshadow the real "fit" he is about to display in the banquet hall. Though the king tries to regain his composure stating that at least the "grown serpent" (Banquo) lies dead, and the worm (Fleance), has "[n]o teeth for the present," Macbeth remains visibly shaken by the news.

When the first murderer leaves, Lady Macbeth seeks out her husband to give the toast, admonishing him that they are not following the rules of hospitality in neglecting their guests. Just as Macbeth is toasting his guests, wishing them a healthy appetite, Banquo's ghost enters the hall, at first unnoticed by Macbeth, and sits in his chair. When it is time to seat himself, Macbeth sees there is not an empty place for him and states "[t]he table's full." Since the others still expect Banquo and cannot see his ghost, they understand that something is terribly wrong with the king. A man consumed with guilt, Macbeth points to the ghost and asks his noble guests, "[w]hich of you have done this?" And this unfounded accusation soon leads to self-incrimination by denying his guilt: "Thou canst not say, I did it: never shake / Thy gory locks at me." The nobleman Ross, recognizing Macbeth's state of mind, tells everyone to rise to leave, but Lady Macbeth asserts her control and save the scene, directing the guests to remain seated, while explaining that her husband often has suffered from "fits" since his youth. She then proceeds to turn on her husband and ridicules his torment for the dire deeds he has wrought in the service of securing his kingship. "This is the very painting of your fear; / This is the air-drawn dagger, which, you said, / Led you to Duncan.... / Shame itself! / Why do you make such faces." Macbeth's response is to challenge the ghost to speak, the effect of which is to cause the image of Banquo to depart temporarily, while to himself, Macbeth laments that "the time has been, /

That, when the brains were out, the man would die, / And there an end; but now, they rise again." In an attempt to regain his composure and add credence to his wife's story, Macbeth tries to explain away his affliction and conceal his deadly deed, telling his guests that he has "a strange infirmity, which is nothing / to those that know me" and glossing over Banquo's absence by drinking to his health. "I drink to th' general joy o' th' whole table, / And to our dear friend Banquo, whom we miss." But the ghost reappears and Macbeth challenges the apparition to assume any other shape than that of a ghost, and he will do battle with it. "Approach thou like the rugged Russian bear, / ... and my firm nerves / Shall never tremble."

This second instance of Macbeth losing control causes Lady Macbeth to chastise her husband once again for spoiling the royal feast. "You have displac'd the mirth, broke the good / meeting / With most admir'd disorder." Macbeth is amazed at her cold and calculating demeanor as she dismisses the guests, directing them to forget social hierarchies and instead depart speedily. "Stand not upon the order of your going, / But go at once." And thus the well-planned, orderly banquet has been transformed to a scene of total chaos. When the guests have departed, the King and Lady Macbeth have a brief conversation that reveals the depth of Macbeth's tortured mind and the belief that he is beyond the point of no return in the crimes he has thus far committed, with no other recourse than to destroy all remaining threats to his power. "I am in blood / Stepp'd in so far, that, should I wade no more, / Returning were as tedious as go o'er." With Banquo gone, he will turn his fear toward Macduff. Macbeth is also desperate to find out his fate, and plans to go tomorrow to consult again with the three witches in whom he has placed his trust. The scene concludes with Lady Macbeth wanting to deceive herself, stating that sleep will cure her husband.

Scene 5 takes place once again on a heath with thunder in the background and the three witches of earlier scenes meet their queen, Hecate, the goddess of witchcraft. Hecate is offended by their lack of respect in their failure to consult with her, a usurpation of her "divine" rights. She voices her complaint in rhymed couplets. "How did you dare / To trade and traffic with Macbeth / In riddles and affairs of death; / And I, the mistress of your charms, / The close contriver of all harms, / Was never called to bear my part, / Or show the glory of our art? She instructs the witches to meet her tomorrow morning at the "pit of Acheron" (the gates of Hell) where Macbeth will seek them out to learn his future. As the queen of witchcraft considers Macbeth to be unworthy, one who "loves for his own ends," she instructs the Weird Sisters to be ready to conjure up their magic spells that will "draw him on to his confusion." Hecate departs, predicting that Macbeth will continue to "spurn fate" and "scorn death."

Scene 6, the conclusion of Act III, takes place at the palace at Forres. It is a brief scene which provides the audience with information on the state of affairs outside the palace walls. Conversing with an unnamed lord (who represents the Scottish citizens), Lennox states that as of late "things have been strangely borne" while it is still generally believed that Malcolm and Donalbain murdered Duncan, their father and that Fleance likewise killed Banquo and fled. He also questions Macduff's absence from the court. But the Lord with whom he speaks has a far different report, namely, that Macduff has gone to England to petition King Edward to enlist the services of Northumberland and Siward and thereby restore Scotland to calm and order. "That by the help of these ... / we may again / Give to our tables meat, sleep to our nights, / Free from our feasts and banquets bloody knives." The scene concludes with Lennox praying for the same restoration to Scotland.

ACT IV

Scene 1 opens with the fourth and final witch scene in the play and is set within a cavern with a boiling cauldron in the middle. The weather is dark and foreboding, with thunder in the background as the three witches brew their "hell-broth" of "fenny snake," "toe of frog," and a long list of similarly disgusting ingredients, and cast spells as they await Macbeth's arrival. While concocting their vile magic potion, they chant their famous song: "Double, double, toil, and trouble: / Fire, burn; and, cauldron, bubble." During these preparations, their queen, Hecate, joins them and compliments them on their efforts, saying, "Oh, well done! I commend your pains, / And everyone shall share i' th' gains." In the midst of their musical celebration, Macbeth enters and greets them as "secret, black and midnight hags," demanding answers to his desperate questions. "Even till destruction sicken, answer me." For their part, the witches are eager to oblige Macbeth and conjure up apparitions to satisfy his demand to know what is in store.

The first apparition appears with a clap of thunder and is nothing more than a head wearing armor, "[h]e will not be commanded." It simply calls out to Macbeth to "beware Macduff" and quickly disappears. The second apparition, again summoned by the thunder, is a child covered with blood and it, too, warns Macbeth, this time to "be bloody, bold, and resolute; laugh to scorn / The power of man, for none of woman born / Shall harm Macbeth." However, this second apparition is also reiterating the deceptive and misleading advice of the three witches in the beginning, the same advice which launched Macbeth's bloody pursuit of the throne. At first, Macbeth is delighted to have this advice reconfirmed, and his first reaction is to spare Macduff's life since he need not fear him. But Macbeth is already caught up in an evil vortex and quickly changes his mind by deciding to murder Macduff—"thou shalt not live." The thunder sounds again, and the third apparition appears, this time as a crowned child carrying a tree in his hand, "[t]hat rises like the issue of a king." This third apparition is the most threatening of all in that it foretells Macbeth's replacement by a new king, one who will restore calm and order. The child gives Macbeth yet another piece of misleading advice in the form of another riddle, telling him to be brave and proud and not to worry about conspirators. "Macbeth shall never vanquish'd be, until / Great Birnam wood to high Dunsinane hill / Shall come against him." This news again reassures Macbeth as he believes that he will never be defeated.

But Macbeth still wants to know the answer to one more question concerning Banquo, namely, whether his "issue ever [will ever] reign in this kingdom?" Though the witches suggest that he does not want to hear the answer to this question, Macbeth protests and boldly threatens them. "I will be satisfied: deny me this, / And an eternal curse fall on you!" Suddenly the cauldron begins to sink, and a trumpet sounds, followed by a procession of eight kings, the last one carrying a mirror which shows him even more kings. But the worst spectacle is that of Banquo's ghost at the end of the procession. As each king passes before his eyes, Macbeth looks in horror and realizes its resemblance to Banquo. "For the blood-bolter'd Banquo smiles upon me, / And points at them for his." Sick at heart that his worst fears will come true, Macbeth curses the witches and all who trust them. "Let this pernicious hour / Stand aye accursed in the calendar!"

Cursing the day, Macbeth calls out to Lennox, who has been waiting outside and tries to ascertain whether he has seen the three weird sisters, and learns that he has not. Nevertheless, Lenox brings him the dread news that Macduff has fled to England. Macbeth is infuriated by the news, vowing to retaliate. "The very firstlings of my heart shall be / The firstlings of my hand." Macbeth intends to take Macduff's castle by surprise and kill his wife and children, and "all unfortunate souls / That trace him in his line."

Scene 2 takes place at Macduff's castle in Fife and opens with Lady Macduff (with her young son at her side) conversing with the noble Ross about her husband's having fled the country. Visibly upset and feeling alone and afraid, Lady Macduff attributes her husband's desertion to madness, calling him a traitor who acted out of fear. Though Ross tries to convince her otherwise, suggesting that it is the times in which they live that are traitorous and that Macduff may have shown great wisdom, he is unable to persuade her. "I pray you, school yourself: but, for your husband, / He is noble, wise, judicious, and best knows / The fits of the season." When the emotionally exhausted Ross leaves, Lady Macduff tells her son that she fears his father is dead. The son, wise beyond his years, refuses to believe her, but asks whether his father is a traitor. When his mother answers that anyone who lies is a traitor and should be hanged by honest men, her son responds with the keen perception of a child's vision that "there are liars and swearers enow to beat the honest men, and / hang them up." While Lady Macduff and her son continue their conversation, they are interrupted by an unknown messenger who has come to warn them "some danger does approach you nearly." The messenger advises her to take the children and flee from Fife and quickly leaves. Tragically, Lady Macduff is too overcome with disbelief and astonishment, which render her paralyzed to act. In truth, however, there really is no time for escape for the murderers are at the door. They enter and her young son puts up a brave defence, calling the first murderer a "shag-hair' villain," and he is quickly stabbed. With his last breath, the young calls out a warning to his mother. "He has kill'd me, mother: / Run away, I pray you!" Lady Macduff, screaming "murder," runs out, pursued by the murderers who are certain to kill her as well.

Scene 3 opens in "a desolate shade" in front of the king's castle in England with Malcolm and Macduff discussing the state of affairs brought about by Macbeth in Scotland. It is most unhappy state of affairs, wherein "[e]ach new morn, / New wisdows howl, new orphans cry; new sorrows / Strike heaven on the face." While Malcolm wants to weep for his homeland, Macduff desires to take up arms against Macbeth. Furthermore, at first the two mean are distrustful of one another. Macduff senses the worry of the prince and assures him that he is not treacherous. Malcolm, however, is still not convinced and proceeds to question Macduff's motives in leaving his wife and child in peril in order to come to England, to which Macduff responds that he has lost all hope. But when Malcolm explains that he is still concerned for his own safety, Macduff is forced to cry out that he believes there is no hope for Scotland unless he can join forces with Malcolm against Macbeth. However, since he knows Malcolm does not trust him, Macduff feels he has to leave. "I would not be the villain that thou think'st / For the whole space that's in the tyrant's grasp."

Malcolm is intent on testing Macduff's trustworthiness, and for that purpose the prince pretends to be an evil person filled with vices who, if compared to Macbeth, would make "Black Macbeth ... seem pure as snow." Macduff responds by stating that hell could never produce such evil to compete with that of Macbeth. Malcolm continues with his testing of Macduff. While agreeing that Macbeth is bloody, avaricious, deceitful and malicious, Malcolm insists that he himself is far worse, claiming that he possesses none of the royal graces. "All the particulars of vice so grafted, / That, when they shall be open'd, black Macbeth / Will seem as pure as snow." He further declares that if he were king, he would "[P]our the sweet milk of concord into Hell, / Uproot the universal peace, confound / All unity on earth." Finally succumbing to Malcolm's pretense, Macduff turns on the prince, pronouncing him unfit to govern Scotland or even to live. He gives up on the fight for his homeland and bids farewell to Malcolm a second time. "These evils thou repeat'st upon thyself / Hath banish'd me from Scotland.—O my breast, /Thy hope ends here!"

Once again Malcolm stops Macduff, praising the latter's integrity of soul and noble passion for Scotland. Admitting to the trickery he has used to test Macduff's purpose, Malcolm professes his own virtue. "At no time broke my faith: would not betray / The Devil to his fellow; and delight / No less in truth, than life." And Macduff is relieved to learn the truth as goodness is beginning to prevail. Malcolm pledges to support Macduff in his attempt to overthrow Macbeth. "What I am truly, / Is thine, and my poor country's, to command." When he tells Macduff that Siward and ten thousand English soldiers are at their command to aid in the fight, Macduff is struck silent by this news, confused between appearances and the reality. When questioned, Macduff attributes his confusion to the same theme that has persisted throughout the play, namely that "such welcome and unwelcome things [happen] at once, 'tis hard to reconcile."

A doctor then passes by to say that King Edward is coming and describes King Edward's power of healing. "To the succeeding royalty he leaves / The healing benediction. With this strange virtue, / He hath a heavenly gift of prophesy" (unlike the prophesies borne of witchcraft). Malcolm explains to Macduff that this holy king, in sharp contrast to the evil Macbeth, also possess the divine gift of prophecy, in sharp contrast to the prophesies delivered by the three Weird Sisters. When Ross enters the scene, having just arrived from Scotland, Macduff inquires first about the state of affairs in Scotland and the fate of his wife and son. Ross at first avoids the news of their murder, but when he hears that Malcolm and Macduff are about to lead an attack on Macbeth, he tells about the king's latest act of brutality, the "savage slaughter" of Macduff's family. Macduff is overcome with grief at his loss and tortured with guilt for having left his family defenseless, but Malcolm encourages him to "make us med'cines of our great revenge, / To cure this deadly grief." Macduff agrees with him. And Scotland, the country they love, is described in the most hideous terms. "Alas, poor country! / Almost afraid to know itself. It cannot / Be called our mother, but our grave.... " Ironically, England, the foreign land, is described as a heavenly place with a holy king.

ACT V

Scene 1 takes place in the castle at Dunsinane with an unnamed lady-in-waiting conversing with a physician about Lady Macbeth's sleepwalking. Having observed the queen for two days and not seeing any incidents as the gentlewoman has described, the doctor begins to doubt her truthfulness. Though he attempts to question her about the things Lady Macbeth has said while sleepwalking, the gentlewoman refuses to answer for fear she will not be believed. Lady Macbeth then enters the scene in a tranced state, unable to see the others even though her eyes are open and pauses to rub her hands, as if washing them. But when she cannot get them clean, she screams, "Out, damned spot! ... Yet who would have thought the old man to have had so much blood in him." She speaks as though Macbeth were present, and in so doing, incriminates both of them in the process and continues by revealing Macbeth's part in the deaths of Banquo and Macduff's family. But her thoughts are constantly interrupted by the image of the blood on her hands, and she asks, "Will these hands ne'er be clean?" The doctor then tells the lady-in-waiting that "[t]his disease is beyond my practice," stating that Lady Macbeth needs a priest more than she needs a physician. But before he departs, he begs to the heavens, "God forgive us all!" Ironically, in reviewing all the murderous crimes that have been committed in the name of securing the throne, which she believed both she and her husband were exempt from accountability, Lady Macbeth has finally been driven to insanity. Though she repeatedly attempts to clean the bloody evidence from her person, the evidence stubbornly remains, just as her guilt can no longer be gainsaid. And, an even more compelling irony is manifested when she is in a somnolent state, her true soul is revealed. Indeed, she becomes a victim of appearances herself: Lady Macbeth imagines that she sees blood upon her hands and tries to wash it away in an attempt to cleanse her soul. Just as the ghosts of Macbeth's victims come back to haunt him and expose his culpability in the public realm, Lady Macbeth's insanity causes her to become like one of the undead herself, teetering between reality and madness.

Scene 2 takes place in the open country near Dunsinane with the impending battle in the background. Drums are beating, flags are flying, and the Scottish soldiers have gathered to prepare for their attack against Macbeth. "Revenge burns in them; for their dear causes / Would, to the bleeding and the grim alarm, / Excite the mortified man." The English army, led by Malcolm, Macduff, and Siward is nearby. As Angus, one of the Scottish lords, announces, "Near Birnam wood / Shall we meet them," reminding us of the last prophecy of the three witches. From the conversation amongst the gentlemen in this scene, the audience learns that Donaldbain has not yet joined his brother Malcolm. The lords also discuss Macbeth's beleagured state. Although the king has fortified his castle, he is bereft of supporters. It is a well known fact that Macbeth has lost self-control, and is generally believed to have gone mad. "He cannot buckle his distemper'd cause / Within the belt of rule." The focus now shifts to the imminent battle which will purging Scotland of its sickness. As the scene closes, they are off to Birnam wood for the fulfillment of the prophecy.

Scene 3 opens with Macbeth trying to calm his fears about the approaching army by remembering the prophecies of the witches. "Till Birnam Wood to Dunsinane, / I cannot taint with fear." He then reminds himself that Macduff was surely born of woman. Finally, he lies to himself one more time in denying his fear of the impending assault. "The mind I sway by, and the heart I bear, / Shall never sag with doubt, nor shake with fear." But a fearful servant interrupts his thoughts, and informs the king that ten thousand English soldiers are marching towards Dunsinane. Macbeth doesn't want to hear the news, sends the servant away and returns to his dismal reflections, exclaiming that "I have lived long enough: my way of life / Is fall'n into the sere" for he knows that old age will not bring him honor, love, or friendship. Nevertheless, he is determined to "fight, till from my bones my flesh be hacked." As he dons his armor, the king turns to the doctor and asks about his wife. The physician reports that she is "troubled with thick-coming fancies." Macbeth begs the doctor to cure her from the same things he so desperately wants to purge from himself. "Canst thou not minister to a mind diseas'd, / Pluck from the memory a rooted sorrow, / Raze out the written troubles of the brain." By way of response, the doctor articulates the only possible cure, a theme that runs throughout *Macbeth*. "The patient must minister to himself," an ability Macbeth has tragically forfeited in his bloody and obsessive pursuit of the throne. Nevertheless, there is a very poignant moment where Macbeth demonstrates true understanding of the state of affairs in Scotland and almost prayerfully asks the doctor to restore it to health. "If thou couldst, Doctor, cast / The water of my land, find her disease, / And purge it to a sound and pristine health." The scene closes pathetically, Macbeth left with only one officer to helping him. Even his armor no longer fits, because Macbeth is no longer the heroic warrior of former days.

Scene 4 takes place in the country near Birnam Wood with the Scottish rebels having joined forces with Malcolm, Macduff, and the English soldiers. Malcolm enters and encourages those around him by saying, "I hope the days are near at hand that chambers will be safe" to sleep in again. He also tells them that many have deserted Macbeth, and only "constrained things whose hearts are absent" serve him. Finally he advises the soldiers to cut boughs off the trees to use as camouflage in their approach to Dunsinane. Then they are off to war. Unlike the previous scene, these soldiers are under the calm encouragement of Malcolm and are both eager and prepared for battle. There is hope that goodness will prevail and a healed Scotland will result.

Scene 5 takes place within the castle at Dunsinane with Macbeth talking to Seton and his soldiers. He is still deceiving himself as he boasts to the others about their defensive position. "Our castle's strength will laugh a siege to scorn." But his empty words are soon interrupted by the jarring sounds of wailing women. Macbeth's response is that he is unaffected by the sounds, having become inured to "slaughterhouse thoughts." However, he does ask Seton why they are crying and at that point learns that they are lamenting his dead queen. Though he expresses no grief at his loss, Macbeth comments on the total emptiness of life in his most famous soliloquy. "Tomorrow, and tomorrow, and tomorrow, / Creeps in this petty pace from day to day, / To the last syllable of recorded time; / And all our yesterdays have lighted fools / The way to dusty death." It is here that Macbeth so eloquently expresses the consequences of his proleptic vision. In his relentless pursuit of securing his future as the King of Scotland, Macbeth has been negligent, and in his refusal to live in the present, he has assured himself an empty life which will lead him to a dusty death, devoid of purpose and meaning with no good works to be remembered by. Instead, his will be "[a] tale / Told by an idiot, full of sound and fury, / Signifying nothing."

Scene 6 takes place just beyond the castle gate of Dunsinane. With Malcolm, Siward, and Macduff conversing as they lead their army forward. Malcolm instructs his troops to throw down the branches from Birnam Wood, for they no longer need camouflage. It is important to note that the army at first approaches under the camouflage of branches, appearing to be something they are not; and in so doing fulfill the witches' prophesy of Dunsinane coming to Birnam Wood. Clearly in control of his forces and having assumed the leadership he rightfully deserves, Malcolm orders Siward and his son to lead the first charge, while he and Macduff follow. Siward sets off, indicating he is well prepared for the fight while Macduff displays the same eagerness, telling his troops to sound the trumpets. "Give them all breath, / Those clamourous harbingers of blood and death."

Scene 7 is fast-paced, filled with military action and the sounds of war. As Macbeth enters the battlefield, wondering aloud what kind of man would not be born of woman, Young Siward enters and asks his name. Hearing Macbeth's response, the young soldier says that "[t]he devil himself could not pronounce a title more hateful to mine ear." Challenging Macbeth to a duel, Young Siward is defeated by the king and Macbeth has won a temporary victory. Macduff then enters in pursuit of the king, waiting to deliver his personal revenge for his family and he calls out to Macbeth. "If thou be'est slain and with no stroke of mine, my wife and children's ghosts will haunt me still." As Macduff continues his search, Siward gives him an update on the battle. The castle has surrendered without a struggle, and many of Macbeth's men have deserted him. It appears the battle is almost over.

As they depart towards the castle in **scene 8**, Macbeth returns to the scene, admitting that while he has contemplated falling on his own sword in order to end the torture of the mind, he has decided to continue the fight. Macduff spies his enemy and calls out. Macbeth, troubled by his bloody crimes, answers by saying, "Turn, Hell-hound, turn! / Of all men else I have avoided thee: / But get thee back, my soul is too much charg'd / With blood of thine already." Ignoring Macbeth's words, Macduff advances and challenges the king to fight. Still believing he is protected by the promise of the witches' prophecy, Macbeth brags to Macduff that he is invulnerable. "I bear a charmed life; which must not yield / To one of woman born. Macduff quickly dispels the charm by informing him to the contrary. "Macduff was from his mother's womb untimely ripped." Upon this last revelation, Macbeth realizes that he is doomed, and curses the witches' trickery. "And be these juggling fiends no more believe'd, / That palter with us in a double sense." Nevertheless, Macbeth finally decides to fight Macduff because the alternative of surrender would be far worse. "I will not yield, / To kiss the ground before young Malcolm's feet." There are still some vestiges of the heroic warrior in the king. Macbeth raises his shield, and they go off fighting.

Malcolm, old Siward, and Ross enter the scene conversing with one another. Malcolm expresses concerned for their friends who are missing in action, while Siward, the veteran soldier, reminds him that there will be deaths in any battle, but fortunately for them, their losses seem small. Then Malcolm specifically mentions that Macduff and young Siward are missing. Ross, again assuming the role of messenger, delivers the bad news that Siward's son "has paid a soldier's debt / [and] like a man he died." His father can release him peacefully to God knowing that he died fighting like a true soldier. Macduff then enters the scene carrying Macbeth's head on a pole. Knowing that the tyrant king is dead, Macduff salutes Malcolm and says, "Hail, King! for so thou art." The noble thanes join in the greeting as the trumpets sound in the background. Malcolm addresses the crowd and immediately takes steps to return sanity to his country and destroy the fear and chaos as he tells the thanes that they will become earls and that they should call home their exiled friends. The chaos of Macbeth has passed, and the wish for peace in Scotland seems possible once again.

Critical Views

HAROLD C. GODDARD ON MACBETH'S DEEDS AND THE SUPERNATURAL

V

Deeds of violence that come exclusively out of the brute in man have no tragic significance and take their place in human memory with the convulsions of nature and the struggle to survive of the lower orders of life. But when a man of imagination—by which I mean a man in whom the image of God is distinct—stoops to crime, instantly transcendental powers rush to the scene as if fearful lest this single deed shift the moral center of gravity of the universe, as a finger may tip an immense boulder that is in delicate equilibrium. Macbeth and Lady Macbeth (as she was at the outset) seem created to stress this distinction. "A little water clears us of this deed," is her reaction to the murder of Duncan.

> Will all great Neptune's ocean wash this blood
> Clean from my hand? No, this my hand will rather
> The multitudinous seas incarnadine,
> Making the green one red,

is his. One wonders whether the supremacy of the moral imagination over the material universe was ever more tremendously expressed than in those four lines. In them, space is, as it were, forever put in its place. When Lady Macbeth, in the end, attains the same insight that is Macbeth's instantly— "all the perfumes of Arabia will not sweeten this little hand"— she does not pass, it is to be noted, to the second part of the generalization. It is this defect in imagination that makes her, if a more pathetic, a less tragic figure than her husband.

The medieval mind, in the tradition of mythology, represented the tragic conflict, which our irreligious age is likely to think of as just a strife between opposing impulses, as a struggle between devils and angels for the possession of man's soul. Devils and angels are out of fashion. But it is not the nomenclature that counts, and the soundness of the ancient conception is being confirmed, under another terminology, in the researches of psychology into the unconscious mind.

Now the unconscious, whatever else or more it may be, is an accumulation of the human and prehuman psychic tendencies of life on the planet, and the unconscious of any individual is a reservoir that contains latently the experience of all his ancestors. This potential inheritance is naturally an inextricable mixture of good and evil. Hence whenever the threshold of consciousness is sufficiently lowered to permit an influx of the unconscious, a terrific tension arises between forces pulling the individual in different or opposite directions. Samuel Butler has given classic expression to this struggle in *Life and Habit*:

> It is one against legion when a creature tries to differ from his own past selves. He must yield or die if he wants to differ widely, so as to lack natural instincts, such as hunger or thirst, or not to gratify them.... His past selves are living in unruly hordes within him at this moment and overmastering him. "Do this, this, this, which we too have done, and found our profit in it," cry the souls of his forefathers within him. Faint are the far ones, coming and going as the sound of bells wafted on to a high mountain; loud and clear are the near ones, urgent as an alarm of fire. "Withhold," cry some. "Go on boldly," cry others. "Me, me, me, revert hitherward, my descendant," shouts one as it were from some high vantage-ground over the heads of the clamorous multitude. "Nay, but me, me, me," echoes another; and our former selves fight within us and wrangle for our possession. Have we not here what is commonly called an *internal tumult*, when dead pleasures and pains tug within us hither and thither? Then may the battle be decided by what people are pleased to call our own experience. Our own indeed!

This passage makes clear why an unmediated polarity is a distinguishing mark of the unconscious and suggests a biological reason for the Delphic character of all true oracles. Every sentence, declares Thoreau, has two sides: "One faces the world, but the other is infinite and confronts the gods." An oracular utterance is merely an extreme form of such a sentence, an incarnation in microcosmic form of the duality Butler depicts. In choosing between its worldly or infernal and its unworldly or celestial meaning, the individual without realizing it recruits an army, the good or bad impulses and acts of millions who have gone before him. Dreams too—many of them—have this ambiguous character and without violence to their imagery can often be taken in contradictory senses. And tragic irony always can. But so hidden may be the second meaning that it requires the future to reveal it, as it may take a second or several readings to uncover it in the printed play.

VI

From end to end, *Macbeth* is packed with these Delphic effects as is no other work of Shakespeare's: words, acts, and situations which may be interpreted or taken in two ways at the peril of the chooser and which in the aggregate produce an overwhelming conviction that behind the visible world lies another world, immeasurably wider and deeper, on its relation to which human destiny turns. As a face now reveals and now conceals the life behind it, so the visible world now hides this other world as does a wall, now opens on it as does a door. In either case it is there—there not as a matter of philosophical speculation or of theological tradition or hypothesis, but there as a matter of psychic fact.

Scholars who dismiss the supernatural element in *Macbeth* as stage convention or condescension to popular superstition stamp themselves as hopelessly insensitive not merely to poetry but to sincerity. Not only the plot and characters of the play, which are up to a certain point the author's inventions, but its music, imagery, and atmosphere—effects only partly under his conscious control—unite in giving the impression of mighty and inscrutable forces behind human life. Only one convinced of the reality of these forces could conceivably have imparted such an overwhelming sense of their presence. Neither could a mere stage contrivance have exercised the influence *Macbeth* has over the imaginations of later poets: Milton, Blake, the Keats of *Hyperion*, Emily Brontë, to name no others. Each sees the poet's vocation, as Shakespeare did in *Macbeth*, as an attempt to reclaim a dark region of the soul. "Shine inward," is the blind Milton's prayer to Celestial Light, "there plant eyes." "To open the immortal Eyes of Man inwards," says Blake, is his great task. "To see as a god sees," cries Keats,

> and take the depth
> Of things as nimbly as the outward eye
> Can size or shape pervade.

Macbeth is a milestone in man's exploration of precisely this "depth of things" which our age calls the unconscious. The very phrase "depth psychology" has been used to differentiate the psychology of the unconscious from shallower attempts to understand the mind.

KENNETH MUIR ON THE PORTER SCENE

Although Pope and Coleridge agreed[1] that the Porter scene was interpolated by the players, enough has been said to indicate its topical significance; and although its topicality is not a proof that Shakespeare wrote it, a further consideration of the scene may establish his authorship, as well as having wider implications about the interpretation of the play.

The scene is theatrically necessary, if only because the actor who plays Macbeth has to wash his hands and change his clothes, and, as Capell suggested, it was necessary 'to give a rational space for the discharge of these actions'. Shakespeare was fully conversant with theatrical necessities and he always bowed to them; but if these were the sole reason for the scene's existence, it might have been added by another hand. Some scene, then, there had to be between the exit of Macbeth and the entrance of Macduff; but this does not explain why Shakespeare should introduce a drunken porter, or one suffering from a hangover, when a sober porter, singing an aubade, as in one of the German versions,[2] might seem to serve as well. 'Comic relief' is a convenient, but question-begging term; for Shakespeare, we might suppose, could have used lyrical relief, if relief were needed. As Coleridge pointed out, Shakespeare never introduced the comic except when it may react on the tragedy by harmonious contrast. A good dramatist does not laboriously create feelings of tension and intensity only to dissipate them in laughter. Sometimes he may use the comic as a laughter-conductor, so as to prevent the audience from laughing at the wrong place and at the wrong things. Lear's sublimity is preserved for us by the Fool. In the present case it is impossible to agree with those critics who suppose that the function of the Porter is to take the present horror from the scene. On the contrary, the effect of the Porter scene is almost the exact opposite: it is there to increase our feelings of horror. We are never allowed to forget throughout the scene that a murder has been committed, and that it is about to be discovered. If we laugh, we never forget.

In his opening words the Porter identifies himself with the Porter of hell-gate,[3] who was expected to make jests, but who was something more than a jester. The plays in which he appears are on the theme of the harrowing of hell in the York, Chester, and Townley cycles, and it has been suggested by two recent critics[4] that the knocking on the gate and the entrance of Macduff recall the entrance of Christ into hell. The Townley porter, named Ribald, when he answers Christ's knocking, calls to Belzebub, as Macbeth's porter asks 'Who's there I'th' name of Belzebub?'

The purpose of recalling this traditional character was complex. First, it transports us from Inverness to the gate of hell, without violating the unity of place: Shakespeare has only to tell us the name of the place we were in before. It is hell because Lady Macbeth has invoked the murdering ministers, because Macbeth has called on the stars to hide their fires, and because hell is a state, not a place, and the murderers might say with Faustus's tempter,

> where we are is hell,
> And where hell is, there must we ever be.

Shakespeare's second reason for recalling the miracle plays was that it enabled him to cut the cable that moored his tragedy to a particular spot in space and time, so that on the one hand it could become universalized, or on the other become contemporary. Macbeth's tragedy might therefore appear as a second Fall, with Lady Macbeth as a second Eve; or it could appear as terrifyingly topical. As S.L. Bethell put it,[5]

> the historical element distances and objectifies what is contemporary, and the contemporary element gives current significance to an historical situation ... The whole atmosphere of treason and distrust which informs *Macbeth* found a parallel in the England of the Gunpowder Plot, so that a passing reference serves to define an attitude both to the Macbeth regime and to contemporary affairs.

The reference to treason in the Porter's speech looks back to the executed Thane of Cawdor, the gentleman on whom Duncan had built an absolute trust; and it looks forward to the dialogue between Lady Macduff and her son, and to the long testing of Macduff by Malcolm, which shows the distrust and suspicion which grow from equivocation. Later in the play, Macbeth complains of

> th'equivocation of the fiend
> That lies like truth:

and of those juggling fiends

> That palter with us in a double sense;
> That keep the word of promise to our ear,
> And break it to our hope.

Indeed, as Dowden pointed out,[6] Macbeth, on his first appearance after the discovery of the murder, is compelled to equivocate; and later in the same scene there is an even more striking equivocation

> Had I but died an hour before this chance,
> I had liv'd a blessed time; for, from this instant,
> There's nothing serious in mortality;
> All is but toys: renown, and grace, is dead;
> The wine of life is drawn, and the mere lees
> Is left this vault to brag of.

The audience knows, as Macbeth himself was to know (though he here intended to deceive) that the words are a precise description of the truth about himself. Macbeth's own equivocation, by an ironical twist, becomes merely an aspect of truth. It is a brilliant counterpart to the equivocation of the fiend that lies like truth: it is the equivocation of the murderer who utters truth like lies. Equivocation therefore links up with one of the main themes of the play, and the equivocator would have earned his place in the Porter scene if Father Garnet had never lived or become involved in the Gunpowder Plot.

Similarly, the unnaturalness of the avaricious farmer is contrasted with the images of natural growth and harvest which are scattered through the play; and he is connected with the equivocator because Garnet went under the alias of Farmer. Even the tailor has his place in the scheme of the play, because of the clothing imagery which is so abundant in it.[7]

Notes

1. Pope's edition of Shakespeare; *Coleridge on Shakespeare*, ed. T. Hawkes (1969), p. 215.

2. Schiller's.

3. W.E. Hales, *Notes and Essays on Shakespeare* (1884), pp. 273–90.

4. John B. Harcourt, 'I pray you remember the Porter', *SQ*, XII (1962), 393 ff.; Glynne Wickham, 'Hell Castle and its Door-Keeper', *SS* 19 (1966), pp. 68–74 (reprinted in *Aspects of Macbeth*); W.A. Armstrong,

Shakespeare's Typology: Miracle and Morality Motifs in 'Macbeth' (1970); Michael J.B. Allen, 'Macbeth's Genial Porter', *ELR*, IV (1974), 326–36, which, drawing on the classical links between porters and genii, suggests that the Porter symbolizes Macbeth's evil genius.

5. S.L. Bethell, *Shakespeare and the Popular Dramatic Tradition* (1944), p. 46. Peter Ure pointed out (*NQ*, 28 May 1949) that the section added by Warner to *Albion's England* in 1606 on the Macbeth story was immediately followed by one on the Gunpowder Plot.

6. E. Dowden, *New Sh. Soc. Trans.* (1874).

7. Spurgeon, *Shakespeare's Imagery* (1935), p. 324. H.L. Rogers has pointed out, *RES* (1965), 44, that the tailor may refer to a man associated in the public mind with the Garnet trial.

A.C. BRADLEY ON THE EFFECT OF DARKNESS

A Shakespearean tragedy, as a rule, has a special tone or atmosphere of its own, quite perceptible, however difficult to describe. The effect of this atmosphere is marked with unusual strength in *Macbeth*. It is due to a variety of influences which combine with those just noticed, so that, acting and reacting, they form a whole; and the desolation of the blasted heath, the design of the Witches, the guilt in the hero's soul, the darkness of the night, seem to emanate from one and the same source. This effect is strengthened by a multitude of small touches, which at the moment may be little noticed but still leave their mark on the imagination. We may approach the consideration of the characters and the action by distinguishing some of the ingredients of this general effect.

Darkness, we may even say blackness, broods over this tragedy. It is remarkable that almost all the scenes which at once recur to memory take place either at night or in some dark spot. The vision of the dagger, the murder of Duncan, the murder of Banquo, the sleep-walking of Lady Macbeth, all come in night-scenes. The Witches dance in the thick air of a storm, or, 'black and midnight hags,' receive Macbeth in a cavern. The blackness of night is to the hero a thing of fear, even of horror; and that which he feels becomes the spirit of the play. The faint glimmerings of the western sky at twilight are here menacing: it is the hour when the traveller hastens to reach safety in his inn, and when Banquo rides homeward to meet his assassins; the hour when 'light thickens,' when 'night's black agents to their prey do rouse,' when the wolf begins to howl, and the owl to scream, and withered murder steals forth to his work. Macbeth bids the stars hide their fires that his 'black' desires may be concealed; Lady Macbeth calls on thick night to come, palled in the dunnest smoke of hell. The moon is down and no stars shine when Banquo, dreading the dreams of the coming night, goes unwillingly to bed, and leaves Macbeth to wait for the summons of the little bell. When the next day should dawn, its light is 'strangled,' and 'darkness does the face of earth entomb.' In the whole drama the sun seems to shine only twice; first, in the beautiful but ironical passage where Duncan sees the swallows flitting round the castle of death; and, afterwards, when at the close the avenging army gathers to rid the earth of its shame. Of the many slighter touches which deepen this effect I notice only one. The failure of nature in Lady Macbeth is marked by her fear of darkness; 'she has light by her continually.' And in the one phrase of fear that escapes her lips even in sleep, it is of the darkness of the place of torment that she speaks.[1]

The atmosphere of *Macbeth*, however, is not that of unrelieved blackness. On the contrary, as compared with *King Lear* and its cold dim gloom, *Macbeth* leaves a decided impression of colour; it is really the impression of a black night broken by flashes of light and colour, sometimes vivid and even glaring. They are the lights and colours of the thunderstorm in the first scene; of the dagger hanging before Macbeth's eyes and glittering alone in the midnight air; of the torch borne by the servant when he and his lord come upon Banquo crossing the castle-court to his room; of the torch, again, which Fleance carried to light his father to death, and which was dashed out by one of the murderers; of the torches that flared in the hall on the face of the Ghost and the blanched cheeks of Macbeth; of the flames beneath the boiling caldron from which the apparitions in the cavern rose; of the taper which showed to the Doctor and Gentlewoman the wasted face and blank eyes of

Lady Macbeth. And, above all, the colour is the colour of blood. It cannot be an accident that the image of blood is forced upon us continually, not merely by the events themselves, but by full descriptions, and even by reiteration of the word in unlikely parts of the dialogue. The Witches, after their first wild appearance, have hardly quitted the stage when there staggers onto it a 'bloody man,' gashed with wounds. His tale is of a hero whose 'brandished steel smoked with bloody execution,' 'carved out a passage' to his enemy, and 'unseam'd him from the nave to the chaps.' And then he tells of a second battle so bloody that the combatants seemed as if they 'meant to bathe in reeking wounds.' What metaphors! What a dreadful image is that with which Lady Macbeth greets us almost as she enters, when she prays the spirits of cruelty so to thicken her blood that pity cannot flow along her veins! What pictures are those of the murderer appearing at the door of the banquet-room with Banquo's 'blood upon his face'; of Banquo himself 'with twenty trenched gashes on his head,' or 'blood-bolter'd' and smiling in derision at his murderer; of Macbeth, gazing at his hand, and watching it dye the whole green ocean red; of Lady Macbeth, gazing at hers, and stretching it away from her face to escape the smell of blood that all the perfumes of Arabia will not subdue! The most horrible lines in the whole tragedy are those of her shuddering cry, 'Yet who would have thought the old man to have had so much blood in him?'

Note

1. 'Hell is murky' (v. i. 35). This, surely, is not meant for a scornful repetition of something said long ago by Macbeth. He would hardly in those days have used an argument or expressed a fear that could provoke nothing but contempt.

CLIFFORD DAVIDSON ON THE TRAGEDY OF MACBETH'S CHARACTER

The road which Macbeth travels "to dusty death" involves him in hypocrisy and deception, which are confirmed by the treason he commits. He is unable to appear in public without the mask which he is forced to wear in order that he might conceal the malice of his heart. He appears to Duncan as an angel of light; inwardly, he is a ravening wolf in the service of darkness. Duncan, "a most Sainted-King" (IV, iii, 125), is deceived by Macbeth's show of holiness but, once the initial crime is completed, the usurper's nature becomes progressively known through his acts. As the Bible and the *Homilies* proclaim, men must be judged "by their frutes" (*Matthew* vii, 10; *Homilies*, p. 398). Immediately after the murder of the king, Macduff and Banquo suspect, but in III, vi Lennox and another lord know more exactly the nature of Macbeth's cunning. Hypocrisy is not able to cover itself entirely with pretended sanctity. Cesare Ripa thus pictures *Hippocrisia* as having the feet of a wolf only partly hidden under her clothes.[3] The truth cannot be hidden; time eventually leads truth out of darkness into light.[4]

The extent of Macbeth's iniquity in pretending to be king of Scotland becomes evident when we recall the Elizabethan and Jacobean ideal of kingship. If rightful kings are called little gods, Macbeth can make no genuine claim to the throne. In fact, his very claim is a blasphemy. William Baldwin writes: "What a fowle shame wer it for any now to take upon them the name and office of God, and in their doinges to shew them selves divyls" (*Mirror for Magistrates*, p. 65). The final devilish state of Macbeth's soul is not to be judged from his beginning, which appears to be good, but from his end. Once caught by the devil's bait, only at the end is he able to express his inward state openly in outward appearance. By Act V, Macbeth has become a stereotyped stage tyrant who is unashamedly malicious. So, like Judas, Saul, and Alexander the Great, his beginning may have been good, but he nevertheless proves to be a persecutor, "resisting the Truth much in the end" (Barlow, *Hierons last fare–well*, pp. 6–7).

The pattern of Macbeth's life is directly opposed to the pattern of sainthood. Instead of leading his life "as in the sight and presence of God, who seeth the hearts, and searcheth the reynes of men," Macbeth attempts to hide his soul's secrets from everyone. Instead of being sincere, he is a "double minded" man.[5] Macbeth lacks that integrity without which "the best graces we seeme to have are counterfeit ..." (Downame, *Lectures on the XV. Psalme*, p. 40). In *Macbeth*, the protagonist's courage is praised in Act I, ii, while in Act V it is evidently only counterfeit courage which doggedly fights on despite the hopelessness of the situation. He is opposed by the truly valiant son of warlike Siward, who, though he falls in battle, is God's soldier. Young Siward has fought the good fight against the agents of tyranny and damnation, and he has been victorious even in death.

Faced with the judgment which Malcolm's soldiers will work against him, Macbeth has little choice except to fight: "Beare-like I must fight the course" (V, vii, 4). His hypocritical behavior has reduced him to the level of bestiality, and now he must die like a beast. Edward Philips admonishes his auditory: "learne ... what an abhominable thing sinne is, and among the rest hypocrisie, that it is able to transforme men into beasts, as resembling them in their qualities."[6] Sin does change Macbeth strangely so that all his former nobility is destroyed or changed into something sub-human. In V, viii, 6, Macduff appropriately calls Macbeth a "Hell-hound." Morally and spiritually, Macbeth has become like the deformed figures in Pieter Brueghel the elder's engravings of the vices.

In one of the engravings by Brueghel, a demon holds a mock crown over the head of *Invidia*. Macbeth's hope and desire to gain the coveted symbol of kingship similarly turn out to be a mockery. If he must sell his eternal jewel to gain an earthly crown, he thereby is frustrating any hope his soul might have of gaining a heavenly crown. And because of the position of the king in the hierarchy, the wearing of the earthly crown by Macbeth can only be a mockery. Only one who shares heavenly hope has the right to reach for the symbolic crown.[7]

Like the crown, the kingly robes which Macbeth wears after the completion of Act II are symbols of kingly authority and position. As symbols, they appear to participate in the sanctity of the office which they represent. Bishop Bilson's coronation sermon (sig. B$_1$) asserts: "Yea the very Robes, which [kings] weare, are sanctified." Kings' robes and other apparel are so holy that "no part of their apparel may be wronged or abused." In *The Mirror for Magistrates*, Buckingham notes the contrast between Richard III's clothing and his heart; he is "with pryncely purple rychely clad, / Yet was his hart wyth wretched cares orefret: / And inwardly with deadly fear beset ..." (p. 327). The outward sign is abused when it is not consistent with the inner reality. In this case, the sign—Macbeth's royal robes—are symbolic of authority and dominion which do not in fact exist. The clothing of the hypocrite is of much greater value than his own worth.

The clothes imagery in *Macbeth* therefore ought to be seen as underlining the theme of hypocrisy in the play. In I, iii, Ross's announcement of Macbeth's new honor and position as Thane of Cawdor is greeted with a question: "Why doe you dresse me in borrowed Robes?" Soon, however, Macbeth will attempt to dress himself in the hope of wearing the crown and kingly robes which rightly belong to Duncan. As things turn out, the Macbeth who dons those kingly garments demonstrates that he is only "a dwarfish Theef"; the title of king hangs "loose about him, like a Giants Robe" (V, ii, 26–28). Unlike Antonio in The Tempest (II, i, 267), who brags that his usurped garments sit well upon him, Macbeth is not able to "buckle his distemper'd cause / Within the belt of Rule" (V, ii, 20–21). His cause is, like the monstrous belly of Falstaff, out of all order, yet he himself is small—much smaller than he was in Act I. Sir Thomas Elyot notes that if one has "an ancient robe" inherited from an ancestor, "let him consider that if the first owner were of more virtue than he is that succeedeth, the robe being worn, it diminisheth his praise to them which knew or have heard of the virtue of him that first owned it" (*The Governor*, p. 105). How much more it must be charged against a man if he has viciously stolen the garment from another! Macbeth, to use the common euphemism for stealing, "borrowed" the kingly garments from Duncan, a man of far greater stature. In no way can he increase his own size so that he might be able to fit the robes he has stolen. The large clothes only emphasize the fact that he is not fit to wear the symbols of rule.

Notes

3. Cesare Ripa, *Iconologia* (Padua, 1611), p. 217.

4. *Veritas folia temporis* is a commonplace, and is discussed by Fritz Saxl in *Philosophy and History*, ed. Raymond Klibansky and H. J. Paton (New York, 1963; reprint of 1936 edition), pp. 197–222. Quite typical is the woodcut following the "Epistle Dedicatorie" in Andrewes's *Wonderfull Combate: Time*, with a scythe in his hand, leads the lady Truth out of a dark cavern.

5. Downame, *Lectures on the XV. Psalme*, pp. 26, 27.

6. Edward Philips, *Certain Godly and Learned Sermons* (London, 1607), p. 113. The first edition of this book was published in 1604. Philips was rector of "Saint Saviours in *Southwarke*."

7. Giotto's *Spes* in the Arena Chapel at Padua is reaching for a heavenly crown, which is being handed to her by an angel. See also Mâle, *Gothic Image*, p. 112.

E.A.J. Honigmann
on the Murderer as Victim

A victim or a villain? Macbeth seems to be both in the murder-scene and, though the mixture differs from moment to moment, throughout the first two acts. This impression partly depends upon the flow of information, which the dramatist can regulate as he chooses. The less an audience understands the more inclined it will be to reserve judgement: in Macbeth the opening scenes are so arranged that we never know quite enough about the hero's guilt, and he captures our sympathetic attention as it were under cover of darkness. Commentators who translate surmise into certainty consequently distort the spectator's relationship with the dramatic character: clarifying what the dramatist deliberately left obscure they give us either a villain or a victim, and falsify the very nature of their experience.

A 'criminal' hero in particular can benefit from the audience's uncertainties. In the opening scenes of Macbeth we are made to wonder about the Weird Sisters, their powers, their connection with Macbeth and Lady Macbeth, and Shakespeare artfully withholds the answers. But not the commentators:

> The Witches ... are not goddesses, or fates, or, in any way
> whatever, supernatural beings. They are old women, poor
> and ragged, skinny and hideous, full of vulgar spite ...
> There is not a syllable in *Macbeth* to imply that they are
> anything but women. But ... they have received from evil
> spirits certain supernatural powers.[4]

If we dissect the play at our leisure all this may well seem true.
In the theatre, however, we can only interpret our impressions
as they come to us, in a fixed order, and, I venture to say, we
never share Bradley's certainty that the Weird Sisters are not
'in any way whatever, supernatural beings.' When the play
begins Macbeth and Banquo can make nothing of them ('What
are these?' 'What are you?'), except that they 'look not like th'
inhabitants o' the earth.' Shakespeare's audience must have
been just as puzzled, for the 'Weird Sisters' were foreign to
English mythology, so much so that Holinshed (from whose
chronicles Shakespeare borrowed the name) felt obliged to give
help: 'the weird sisters, that is (as ye would say) ye Goddesses
of destinie.' As the play progresses we learn that Banquo thinks
them 'the instruments of darkness' (I. 3. 124), and that they
acknowledge spirits as their 'masters' (IV. 1. 63). But their exact
status remains undefined, except that they are closely associated
with an 'unknown power' (IV. 1. 69). They may be witches, but
we cannot take even this for granted:[5] and at the beginning of
the play, when we feel our way into Macbeth's mind, a
spectator uncontaminated by criticism must think of them as
sui generis, a mystery.

The mystery extends to their relationship with Macbeth.
Dover Wilson assures us that 'Macbeth exercises complete
freedom of will from first to last'.[6] Another critic wrote, more
cautiously, that 'Macbeth makes no bargain with the emissaries
of the powers of darkness; nor are they bargainable. The
knowledge offers itself to him: it is, indeed, as he says, "a
supernatural soliciting". But he is not solicited to the treachery
and murder which he commits.'[7]

True, as long as we can be certain that there is no
connection between the Weird Sisters and Lady Macbeth. But

if Moelwyn Merchant was correct in saying that 'it is surely unnecessary to argue today that Lady Macbeth's invocation of "the spirits that tend on mortal thoughts" ... is a formal stage in demonic possession',[8] then Lady Macbeth solicits her husband on behalf of the Weird Sisters. She does so, it should be observed, by hailing him by his three titles, just like the Sisters—

> Great Glamis! Worthy Cawdor!
> Greater than both, by the all-hail hereafter!

She continues where they left off. The Weird Sisters strike first, then Lady Macbeth assaults him in his imagination, blow after blow, and her words have an even more fearful effect—so that theirs seems a joint attack, master-minded from afar. And even if not formally 'possessed', Lady Macbeth appears to be somehow in league with evil and Macbeth its victim, a fly in the spider's web who struggles mightily but cannot escape.

'Somehow' in league may sound vague, but we must beware of asserting more than we can prove where the Weird Sisters are concerned. Somehow they make contact with Macbeth's mind, even before he sees them: his very first words, 'So foul and fair a day I have not seen', suggest their influence, since he unconsciously echoes their earlier chant. And as they somehow give Banquo 'cursed thoughts' in his dreams (II. 1. 8), and can invade the sleeping mind, what are we to make of the dagger that seems to marshal Macbeth to Duncan's chamber a mere thirteen lines later? Another cursed thought, planted in Macbeth's mind to draw him to the murder? All of these impressions work together, suggesting that the Weird Sisters have access to the human mind (Lady Macbeth, Banquo, Macbeth), and can attack Macbeth's directly and indirectly.

Yet these impressions never harden into certitude. Neither the very first scene, which was dropped by Tyrone Guthrie because he mistakenly thought it assigned a 'governing influence'[9] to the Weird Sisters, nor any other scene proves beyond doubt that Macbeth is just a victim. The dramatic perspective merely inclines us to fear for him. Shakespeare stimulates an anxiety for the hero, before the murder. Similar to the audience's protective anxiety for Othello, even though Macbeth's intentions are more straightforwardly criminal than the Moor's. A single passage may illustrate the dramatic advantages Lady Macbeth's allusion to an earlier meeting when her husband broke 'this enterprise to me' (I. 7. 47ff.). On the strength of this passage some editors have postulated lost scenes or an earlier version of the play.[10] Had the audience actually witnessed a scene where 'the husband and wife had explicitly discussed the idea of murdering Duncan at some favourable opportunity',[11] we must reply, Shakespeare would not have been able to arouse the required response, the sense that Lady Macbeth exaggerates her husband's guilt. Such a discussion would have left no room for doubt, whereas Lady Macbeth's oblique, reference to a previous meeting, in a speech that begins so oddly, exists only to beget doubt.

What *beast* was't then
That made you break this enterprise to me?
When you durst do it, *then you were a man* ...

The tendency to overstatement and emotionalism is as marked as, after the murder, her understatement and emotional deadness. Accordingly, though we believe in a previous meeting, we cannot trust her account of it. She *says* that he broke the enterprise to her and swore to carry out the murder, but we have seen how she puts her ideas into his mind ('Hie thee hither / That I may pour my spirits in thine ear'[12]) and, though Macbeth lets her words pass unchallenged, we distrust all that she asserts. Her speech, in effect, makes Macbeth not more but less guilty; we hear her say that he proposed the murder but, not knowing what really happened, we overreact to her emotionalism and think him the more likely to be innocent.

Notes

4. Bradley, *Shakespearean Tragedy*, p. 341.

5. The theatre-audience might well suspect the Weird Sisters of being

witches but could not be certain of it—not, at least, in Act I, where it matters most. Though they are called witches in the Folio stage-directions (which are the work of a copyist, not necessarily Shakespeare's own words), the audience had no access to this text and could not be misled by it. Nor would it be misled by the rump-fed ronyon who allegedly addressed one of the Weird Sisters as 'witch' (I. 3. 6), since this was a common term of abuse, not always used discriminatingly. More significant is the fact that Macbeth and Banquo never identify them as witches, and that Simon Forman, who saw the play at the Globe in 1611, called them not witches but '3 women feiries or Nimphes.'

6. Dover Wilson (ed.), *Macbeth*, p. xxi.

7. J.M. Murry, *Shakespeare* (1948 ed.) p. 326.

8. W. Moelwyn Merchant, in *Shakespeare Survey*, xix (1966) 75.

9. Carlisle, *Shakespeare from the Greenroom*, p. 346.

10. See Dover Wilson (ed.), *Macbeth*, pp. xxxivff.

11. Bradley, *Shakespearean Tragedy*, p. 480.

12. I. 5. 23.

JOHN RUSSELL BROWN ON IMAGES OF DEATH

Superficially, *Macbeth* seems to return to a more conventional mode, and on one level it is much more straightforwardly a play about an ambitious prince who overreaches himself in murdering the King; and who brings about his own downfall in the end. But it goes beyond Shakespeare's earlier treatments of the theme, notably in two ways. One is the new dimension given by the witches, and the sense of evil which is generated largely through their presence in the play; for this enables Shakespeare to show a more profound spiritual change in Macbeth than in any of his earlier protagonists. Bolingbroke and Claudius feel their guilt, but Macbeth is shown as creating his own hell. In this the play has links with Marlowe's *Doctor Faustus*, but whereas Faustus achieves nothing in return for selling his soul, and in the end, terrified at the prospect of punishment, is whisked off by devils into a traditional stage hell-mouth, Shakespeare expresses dramatically through his presentation of Macbeth that subtler idea of hell verbalised in

Mephistopheles' description of it as 'being depriv'd of everlasting bliss' (Scene III, l.82). Faustus himself seems to begin to understand this in his curses at the end:

> curse Lucifer
> That hath depriv'd thee of the joys of heaven;
>> (Scene XIX, ll.181–2)

but in Marlowe's play hell as deprivation remains merely a concept. It remained for Shakespeare to realise on stage what this means in terms of character.

A second way in which Shakespeare breaks new ground in *Macbeth* is in his deeper study of the nature of ambition, which is the special concern of this essay. Ambition is usually understood in its straightforward sense as an eagerness to gain promotion and power, to rise in the world, and, as Duncan's general in the field, Macbeth might be expected to fit Bacon's conception in 'Of Ambition': 'Good Commanders in the Warres, must be taken, be they never so *Ambitious* ... And to take a Soldier without *Ambition*, is to pull off his Spurres.' Charles Lamb saw further than this in a striking comment provoked by the actor G.F. Cooke's playing of Richard III as a 'very wicked man' who kills for pleasure:[1]

> The truth is, the Characters of Shakespeare are so much the objects of meditation rather than of interest or curiosity as to their actions, that while we are reading any of his great criminal characters—Macbeth, Richard, even Iago,—we think not so much of the crimes which they commit, as of the ambition, the aspiring spirit, the intellectual activity, which prompts them to overleap those moral fences.

Lamb was led to notice something especially significant in *Macbeth*—that the emphasis when we *read* the play is less on what he does than on the activity of mind connected with his deeds. Lamb strikingly linked, perhaps equated, ambition, aspiration and intellectual activity, in a way which now may seem a little eccentric. For on the one hand, the meaning of ambition is more restricted than this on the one occasion when Macbeth speaks the word, at that point towards the end of Act I when he comes nearest to abandoning the murder of Duncan. At this moment of revulsion against the killing of the King,

We will proceed no further in this business,

(I.vii.31)

Macbeth reduces all that has been exciting him in the contemplation of the death of Duncan to 'only vaulting ambition', the mere desire to be King. This would seem to justify the claim that[2]

Macbeth has not a predisposition to murder; he has merely an inordinate ambition that makes murder itself seem to be a lesser evil than failure to achieve the crown.

On the other hand, Lamb's comment reduces to a subordinate role the moral issues which to many have seemed of primary importance. The play has been seen as effectively a morality, with an action that can be summarised thus:[3]

Its hero is worked upon by forces of evil, yields to temptation in spite of all that his conscience can do to stop him, goes deeper into evil-doing as he is further tempted, sees the approach of retribution, falls into despair, and is brought by retribution to his death.

This way of regarding *Macbeth* as an exemplary play displaying the degeneration of a great criminal who has 'no morally valid reason for killing Duncan',[4] has satisfied many, although it does not account for a sense that somehow, in spite of everything! Macbeth retains an heroic stature at the end, when 'in the very act of proclaiming that life "is a tale told by an idiot, *signifying nothing*" personal life announces its virtue, and superbly, *signifies itself.*'[5] Lascelles Abercrombie's extraordinary use here of the word 'virtue' may be related to Wilson Knight's view that Macbeth 'has won through by excessive crime to an harmonious and honest relation with his surroundings.... He now knows himself to be a tyrant confessed, and wins back ... integrity of soul.'[6]

The word 'ambition' is used only three times in the play, and always in simple relation to the idea of worldly power, of gaining the throne, as when Lady Macbeth says her husband is 'not without ambition' (I.v.16), or Ross explains the supposed guilt of Malcolm and Donalbain for the death of Duncan in terms of 'thriftless ambition' (II.iv.28). The compulsion that drives Macbeth is more complex than this, and requires further analysis. A better understanding of why Macbeth does what he does may in turn help to explain the curious contradictions that tend to emerge in the common moralistic accounts of the play, which are torn between condemning him as a criminal and rescuing a grandeur, integrity, even virtue for him at the end. A sense of this difficulty has in part prompted a recent account of Macbeth as lacking 'the requisite moral sense and agony of conscience that any proper tragic hero must have';[7] this is a response to critics who see Macbeth as essentially good, when he has 'neither moral sense nor awareness of its existence'.[8] Such an account of Macbeth may seem a strange, even perverse, reading, but it stems from a genuine problem, and involves an important recognition that Macbeth's 'imagination is not under his control; he is its creature.'[9] For another common assumption about Macbeth is that because he has great poetry to speak he must be an 'intellectual giant',[10] when a very important question the text raises is how far Macbeth understands his own words.

Notes

1. *Charles Lamb on Shakespeare*, ed. Joan Coldwell (New York, 1978), p. 35.

2. *Macbeth*, ed. Kenneth Muir (1951), Introduction, p. lvi.

3. Willard Farnham, *Shakespeare's Tragic Frontier* (Berkeley and Los Angeles, 1950, reprinted 1963), p. 79.

4. Matthew N. Proser, *The Heroic Image in Five Shakespearean Tragedies*

(Princeton, 1965); p. 52. Proser is interested in the inadequacy of such a comment to explain Macbeth's deeds, and he too finds the centre of the play's complexity in Macbeth himself, emphasising the manliness required of the soldier-hero, and describing the action in terms of a conflict between conscience and desire; for him Macbeth moves 'toward enacting without moral reservation—the ethic of pure desire' (p. 74).

5. Lascelles Abercrombie, *The Idea of Great Poetry* (1925), p. 178; see also R.A. Foakes, 'Macbeth' in *Shakespeare Select Bibliographical Guides*, ed. Stanley Wells (1973), pp. 190–3.

6. *The Wheel of Fire* (1930); pp. 171–2. In his fine account of *Macbeth*, relating it to Marlowe's *Doctor Faustus*, Wilbur: Sanders takes off from Abercrombie and Wilson Knight in trying, to 'avoid separating the act of judgment which *sees through* Macbeth, from the act of imagination which sees the world *with* him', and finds, in the courage and honesty of his bearing in facing 'the realities of his situation' at the end, an important positive element, in a 'tremulous equilibrium between affirmation and despair'; see *The Dramatist and the Received Idea* (Cambridge, 1968), pp. 299–307.

7. Bertrand Evans, *Shakespeare's Tragic Practice* (Oxford, 1979), p. 221.

8. *Ibid.*, p. 215.

9. Ibid., p. 219.

10. Richard David, *Shakespeare in the Theatre* (Cambridge, 1978), p. 95; David, in contrast to Abercrombie, Proser, Wilson Knight and Sanders, thinks that after the early part of the play 'there is little for Macbeth to do but decline' (p. 92), and praises Laurence Olivier's performance in the part for the sense it conveyed of 'enormous undeveloped capabilities', as opposed to Ian McKellen's playing of it, which did nothing of the kind.

WILLIAM EMPSON ON THE MEANING
OF EQUIVOCATION

The only standard argument for putting *Macbeth* later than *Lear* seems to be the Porter's joke about equivocation, which is held to be a direct reference, beyond doubt, to the trial of the leading Jesuit Garnet from the end of March 1606 onwards (that is, none of the other arguments seem to me decisive). One cannot simply reply that the joke was added when it was topical, because it fits in with so major a cry as Macbeth saying

"I now begin / To doubt the equivocation of the fiend", let alone minor phrases which merely echo the story; they cannot all have been added later, because that assumes a dramatist who didn't know what he was writing about to start with. However, I think it is dangerous in this process of dating to neglect the element of luck; in fact it seems fair to be rather superstitious about the luck of a man of genius, in such matters, because he can feel somehow what is going to become "topical". Obviously the idea that equivocation is important and harmful and above all protean did not simply become discovered at the trial of Garnet; it would be as plausible to say that the trial went off as it did because that was felt (these state trials of course were as elaborately prepared beforehand as any in recent history). The echoes of the Shakespeare play in other people's plays, usually called in evidence, come very soon after the trial—while it was topical; provokingly soon if you want to argue that Shakespeare had rushed out his masterpiece in between. Indeed the current theory, as I understand, makes him not merely write it but prepare it for a Court performance (with elaborate business presumably) between May and early August of 1606; surely that amount of pace is too hot. And on the other hand none of these echoes come early enough to support the pre-equivocation draft of 1602 posited by Dover Wilson. I think Shakespeare simply got in first with this topic, in 1605, and did not have to add anything to make it look startlingly topical in its second year. It was already about what was really happening; for that matter, I should think it just comfortably predated the actual Gunpowder Plot affair.

By the way, Dover Wilson's argument that the prattle of the child Macduff must be a later insertion intended as a reference to the Garnet trial (because he says a traitor means one who "swears and lies") does seem to me absurd. The argument is that the child uses the word in a different sense from that of Ross, who has just said it, so the effect is artificial and can't have been in the first draft; but obviously children often do do that. This seemed to need fitting in here, but I wish to avoid fussing about trivialities; probably no one would deny that there may have been cuts and insertions by Shakespeare. The very specific proposals of Dover Wilson about what was cut are what I want to examine here.

In the first place, he feels that the murder of Duncan comes too quickly, or anyway abnormally quickly; the hesitation of Macbeth is a key dramatic effect which in most plays would be given space. This is true, but the whole point about Macbeth is that he is hurried into an ill-considered action, or that he refuses to consider it himself: "let not light see"—"the eye wink at the hand"—"which must be acted ere they may be scanned"; the play is crowded with such phrases, and its prevailing darkness is a symbol of his refusal to see the consequences of his actions. These consequences are to be long drawn out, but the choice of killing Duncan is to be shown as the effect of two or three shocks close together. Dover Wilson proposes whole scenes to be added before the murder of Duncan, and I think this would not merely be less "exciting" but off the point of the play. A. C. Bradley, to be sure, has said this already, but I don't think he recognised enough the "psychology" as the contemporary audience would see it, which was rather what we now call "existentialist". Problems about free will, which are raised particularly sharply by prophetic witches, were much in the air, and also the idea of the speed with which the self-blinded soul could be damned. One might perhaps imagine that Shakespeare cut down his first version to get the right effect, but that he really intended the effect, and wasn't merely pushed into it by a Court performance, seems hard to doubt.

Some remarks by Dover Wilson on the state of mind of Macbeth, which only bear indirectly on the question of cuts, had better be looked at next. Murderous thoughts, we are told, first come to him, not before the play nor yet on hearing the prophecy, but on hearing that he has become Thane of Cawdor so that half of the prophecy has been fulfilled. The temptation fills him with horror: "the symptoms would be meaningless" unless he were "an innocent spirit reeling under an utterly unforeseen attack". This first assault of the Tempter is viewed in moral terms, and Macbeth repels it as such, but the idea continues to "mine unseen". When Duncan appoints Malcolm his heir, though the deed seems as terrible as ever, Macbeth "has moved appreciably nearer to it". I should have thought he clearly plans to do it: the words are:

> Stars, hide your fires;
> Let not light see my black and deep desires:
> The eye wink at the hand: yet let that be
> Which the eye fears, when it is done, to see.

The chief thought here, surely, as in all these habitual metaphors of darkness, is that Macbeth wants somehow to get away from or hoodwink his consciousness and self-knowledge and do the deed without knowing it. His first meeting with his wife helps forward this process, as Dover Wilson agrees. But by the stage of the I.vii soliloquy ("if it were done ...") he has reached "a new stage of his disease"; he is thinking not morally but purely from self-interest, says Dover Wilson. Yet "the voice of the good angel can still be heard by us, though not by Macbeth, speaking through the poetry which reveals his subconscious mind". (A. C. Bradley ought to be given credit here, I think.) The proof that his objections are now only prudential is that those are the only ones he makes to his wife (but they are the only ones he *dares* make) and this is why he is won over by her plan to hide the murder—though obviously open to suspicion, it gives him "the talisman his soul craves", an *appearance* of safety (so far from that, it seems to me, what wins him over is her reckless courage). After the murder he has no morality but only bad dreams of being assassinated, which drive him on from crime to crime (but it is the suppressed feeling of guilt, surely, which emerges as neurotic fear—that is *how* he is "possessed", if you regard him as possessed).

ROBERT S. MIOLA ON SOME SENECAN CONVENTIONS

Similarities between Shakespeare's two tyrant tragedies, *Richard III* and *Macbeth*, have long been observed. An early essay in the

British Magazine (1760) remarked that both plays treated the same subject, ambition;[37] later in the eighteenth century there arose a lively debate concerning the courage of the main characters. Comparing Richard and Macbeth at length, John Philip Kemble concluded: 'Richard's character is simple, Macbeth's mix'd. Richard is only intrepid, Macbeth intrepid, and feeling.' This pithy distinction echoes in various formulations throughout the centuries and, it may be noted, in the present study. Other critics have pointed to the considerable verbal and structural parallels between these two plays.[38] And, as is often noticed, both *Richard III* and *Macbeth* have origins in Renaissance chronicle, medieval drama, and Senecan tradition.[39] Earlier drama, frequently illustrating the workings of sin, conscience, and providential order, provides a means of structuring loose chronicle into tyrant tragedy. Seneca again contributes paradigms of rhetoric, characterization, and design—potent configurations of tragic language and idea. *Macbeth* represents in some ways an advance from *Richard III*: it exhibits a smoother integration of its various constituents and a more sophisticated recension of Senecan elements, one which purposefully defies its classical models by various strategies of contradiction and dissonance.

Perhaps the most frequently remarked, and most frequently dismissed, remembrance of Seneca in this play is Macbeth's 'Things bad begun make strong themselves by ill' (III. ii. 55), a recasting of the well-known sentence, 'per scelera semper sceleribus tutum est iter' (*Ag.* 115).[40] The sentence perhaps recurs again later: 'I am in blood / Stepp'd in so far that, should I wade no more, / Returning were as tedious as go o'er' (III. iv. 135–7). Important in all versions is the monomaniacal absoluteness, the grim dedication to self, the lure of the forbidden unknown, the irresistible drive onward, and most significant, the hierophantic elevation of *scelus*. As we have observed earlier, the general popularity of the maxim provides evidence not of specific indebtedness but of intercultural appropriation; it illustrates concisely what Seneca meant to posterity. The tag was so familiar an element of theatrical vocabulary that it provided a pivot for this comic by-play in Marston's *The Malcontent* (1604):

> MENDOZA. Then she's but dead; 'tis resolute she dies;
> *Black deed only through black deed safely flies.*
> MALEVOLE. Pooh! *Per scelera semper sceleribus tutum est iter.*
> MENDOZA. What! Art a scholar? Art a politician? Sure
> thou art an arrant knave. (V. iv. 13–17)

In more serious contexts the maxim serves instantly to characterize the speaker—usually a tyrant like Richard, who also uses a variation (IV. Ii. 63–4), or Macbeth—as passionate in will and grimly dedicated to evil. In addition, Cunliffe (p. 82) and others note the recurrence of another Senecan maxim, 'curae leues locuntur, ingentes stupent' (*Phae.* 607, 'light griefs speak, heavy ones are mute'), in Malcolm's 'Give sorrow words. The grief that does not speak / Whispers the o'er fraught heart, and bids it break' (IV. Iii. 209–10). This passage echoes meaningfully in Macbeth's wish for an antidote to 'Cleanse the stuff'd bosom of that perilous stuff / Which weighs upon the heart' (V. iii. 44–5). These two Senecan maxims, the one describing a dynamic, irresistible *scelus*, the other a sorrow beyond words, stake out the spiritual territory Macbeth traverses throughout the play.

The rhetoric of illful Senecan protagonists elsewhere characterizes the Scottish tyrant. Shakespeare several times employs the night topos familiar from *Hamlet*—Lucianus' grim nocturne and Hamlet's own soliloquy, ''Tis now the very witching time of night' (III. ii. 388 ff.). On the Renaissance stage such lucubrations often take the form of invocations; witness a passage from a domestic tragedy acted by the Lord Chamberlain's Men, *A Warning for Fair Women* (1599):

> Oh sable night, sit on the eie of heaven,
> That it discerne not this blacke deede of darknesse,
> My guiltie soule, burnt with lusts hateful fire,
> Must wade through bloud, t'obtaine my vile desire.

Be then my coverture, thicke ugly Night,
The light hates me, and _I_ doe hate the light. (910–15)

Noting this kind of rhetoric in Marlowe and Munday, Braden
charts its variations in _Macbeth_.[41] Macbeth calls on the stars to
hide their fires, 'Let not light see my black and deep desires' (I.
Iv. 50–1). Lady Macbeth intones an eerie invocation, 'Come,
thick Night, / And pall thee in the dunnest smoke of hell' (I. V.
50–1). Later, planning the murder of Banquo, Macbeth echoes
his wife: 'Come, seeling night, / Scarf up the tender eye of
pitiful day' (III. ii. 46–7). One need not argue for specific sources
to recognize important continuities. The conspiratorial night
becomes the literal setting for horrid action in both _Thyestes_ and
Agamemnon. Seneca uses the night topos to express man's
limitless power for evil; in _Macbeth_ Shakespeare, probably
inspired immediately by Holinshed's description of a six-month
black-out following the murder (Bullough, vii. 483–4), uses it to
suggest an implicit moral order, one that registers shock at
man's wickedness and threatens consequences.

(...)

As we have seen before, Shakespeare continually experiments
with Senecan conventions as well as rhetoric, transforming
them to his own uses. In _Richard III_ Tyrrel, about to play
messenger to the king, announces the murder of the princes to
the audience in a soliloquy that reveals his own guilt and
remorse. In _Macbeth_ the murder of children again forces the
nuntius from his conventional role into a heightened moral
awareness. Risking his own life, a messenger enters and warns
Lady Macduff and her family of imminent danger:

I doubt some danger does approach you nearly.
If you will take a homely man's advice,
Be not found here. (IV. Ii. 67–9)

This homely man contrasts sharply with the conventional
nuntius, especially the one who appears earlier in the form of

the bleeding Captain.[45] Like his Senecan prototypes, the Captain reports on action witnessed off stage, speaking in a lurid diction that mingles reliable objectivity and personal fascination. The later messenger, by contrast, foretells action, delivering a message not from another but from himself. No neutral functionary, this humble, nameless man takes a moral stand at considerable personal risk. (He is dressed as a priest in Welles's 1948 film.) Such a messenger, though late and compromised by his early exit, demonstrates the freedom of the individual human will and serves as part of the larger reaction against the threatening evil.

Notes

37. Vickers, iv. 416; the quotation from Kemble below appears in vi. 435. For the debate see also vi. 407 ff., 447 ff., 462 ff.

38. See e.g. Fred Manning Smith, 'The Relation of "Macbeth" to "Richard the Third"', *PMLA* 60 (1945), 1003–20; Jones (1971, 200 ff.) suggests that Gloucester's career in *3 Henry VI* and *Richard III* provides a structural model for *Macbeth*.

39. On Holinshed see Muir, 209–110, 215–16; Bullough, vii. 447–51. On medieval traditions see Glynne Wickham, 'Hell-Castle and its Door-Keeper', *ShS* 119 (1966), 68–74; John B. Harcourt, "'I Pray You, Remember the Porter'", *SQ* 12 (1961), 393–402; Felperin, 118–44; Jones (1977), 79–83; McRoberts (n. 30 above), 163–8. For the suggestion that Shakespeare had been reading Seneca at the time of *Macbeth* see Thomson, 119–24; Bullough, vii. 451–5; Muir, 211–14. An occasionally useful study, marred by a tendency to generalize and to overlook the chronicles, is that of Paul Bacquet, '*Macbeth* et l'influence de Sénèque', *Bulletin de la Faculté des Lettres de Strasbourg* (1961), 399–411.

40. See e.g. Bullough, vii. 452.

41. 'Senecan Tragedy and the Renaissance', *ICS* 9 (1984), 277–92.

45. On the Captain's Senecan speech see J.M. Nosworthy, 'The Bleeding Captain Scene in *Macbeth*', *RES* 22 (1946), 126–30; Bulman, 170–1.

Shakespeare's greatest parts for women naturally cluster at periods when the playwright had an outstanding boy actor, and the lead boy in 1606–97 had three choice parts in a row— Shakespeare's Lady Macbeth and Cleopatra, as well as Barnes's Lucretia in *The Devil's Charter*.[2] (The actor may, in fact, have had a fourth great role if the view that a boy played the Fool in *Lear* is right.)[3]

Who was that boy? All the evidence points to John Rice. He was singled out, along with the lead adult actor Richard Burbage, to appear before the King in an ambitious program financed by the Merchant Taylors of London in the summer of 1607.[4] Rice was elaborately costumed for the occasion.[5] Though his speech—specially composed by Ben Jonson—only ran to twelve lines, brilliant delivery was important to the spectacle. Rice's master, John Heminges, was paid forty shillings "for his direction of his boy that made the speech to His Majesty," while the boy got five shillings.[6]

(...)

This clustering of Rice's roles' with a witch-like aspect (Lucretia Borgia, Cleopatra, Lady Macbeth) would seem to support those who consider Lady Macbeth the "fourth witch" of the play.[12] Directors have emphasized her evil nature by associating her with the witches visually, or even by having her double the role of Hecate.[13] It is true that she invokes Night and "murth'ring ministers" (demons—just as her husband invokes Night and Hecate. Her evil ministers are clearly the fallen counterparts of angelic "ministers of grace" called on by Hamlet (1.4.39).[14]

In fact, Lady Macbeth's grand invocation at 1.5.40–54 is full of "witch talk." She orders the evil spirits to "unsex me here"— and witches were famously unsexed, a fact emphasized in *Macbeth*'s three witches, played by men. Banquo remarks on their beards at 1.3.45–47, as Hamlet does on the boy actor who had grown up to adult (bearded) parts at *Hamlet* 2.2.423. The witches' sexual traffic with devils was considered one consequence of their loss of sexual attractiveness for men. Lady Macbeth plays with the idea of that sexual traffic with devils when she calls the demons: "Come to my woman's breasts / And take my milk for gall."[15] Witches nursed their familiars from their "marks," considered as teats for diabolic nourishment. Since the marks were often near witches' "privy parts," the nursing could be a kind of foreplay preceding intercourse.[16] La Pucelle calls on her familiars with a reminder how "I was wont to feed you with my blood" (*1 Henry VI* 5.3.14).[17] Joan's familiars, when they abandon her, refuse the offered teats, unlike other familiars, who feed onstage. In *The Witches of Edmonton*, the dog-familiar is seen sucking a mark on Mother Sawyer's arm (2.1.147), and another character describes the way he will "creep under an old witch's coats and suck like a great puppy" (5.1.173–74). Mother Sawyer says her mark has dried up, and asks the dog (4.1.157–60) to

> Stand on thy hind legs—up, kiss me, my Tommy,
> And rub some wrinkles on my brow
> By making my old ribs shrug for joy
> Of thy fine tricks. What hast thou done? Let's tickle!

Hecate, who is a witch not a goddess in Middleton's *The Witch*, calls to her familiar, the actor in a cat costume (3.3.49–50):

> Here's one come down to fetch his dues—
> A kiss, a coil [hug], a sip of blood.

She has had sex with this familiar (1.2.96–97). In *The Late Lancashire Witches*, a witch is asked, "Hath thy puggy [little Puck] yet suck'd upon thy pretty duggy?" (line 2017).

The image of witches giving suck to animals was deep in the lore of Shakespeare's time.[18] Some resist having Lady Macbeth use this image; but we should remember that John Rice's other part at the time, Cleopatra, involved a witch-like comparison of the serpent's bite to an animal familiar's sucking (*Antony* 5.2.309–10):

> Dost thou not see my baby at my breast
> That sucks the nurse asleep?

Even before her cry to the evil spirits, Lady Macbeth was associated with an animal familiar. Hearing a caw from offstage, she says: "The raven himself is hoarse / That croaks the fatal enterance of Duncan / Under my battlements" (1.5.38–40).[19] His entry is fatal, as Hecate works "Unto a dismal and a fatal end" (3.5.21). The raven was a regular "familiar," and its loud cry from offstage had special theatrical effect. Indeed, one of the more spectacular sound effects of the Elizabethan stage was the massive cawing of ravens that fulfilled a prophecy and defeated an army in *Edward III*, a play to which Shakespeare may have contributed.[20]

It is likely that we have already heard the raven that crows over Lady Macbeth's castle. In the opening scene, when familiars summon their witches away, two spirits are named— Graymalkin, a cat, and Paddock, a toad. The third witch answers *her* spirit's call, "Anon." The raven's cry was too (yes) *familiar* to make identification necessary. At 4.1.3, the third witch's animal is addressed as Harpier, an apparent nickname based on Harpy. The raven was a harpy, a food-snatcher.[21] When carrion birds settled on corpses, popular fear and loathing depicted them as witches' familiars gathering body parts. The witch literature fostered that belief. In Ben Jonson's *The Sad Shepherd*, a raven waits as huntsmen corner a deer, and its witch is later seen in a chimney corner with a morsel the bird delivered to her.[22] In *The Masque of Queens*, Jonson translated a passage from Lucan, in which a witch waits for a raven to snatch flesh off a corpse and then takes it from the raven.[23] The raven is a particularly unclean bird, whose very presence acts as a curse on a house, as Othello notes (4.1.20–22):

> It comes o'er my memory
> As doth the raven o'er the' infectious house
> Boding to all.

Thersites, when he dreams of cursing, does so as a raven in his own mind: "I would croak like a raven, I would bode, I would bode" (*Troilus* 5.2.191). Caliban uses the raven when he curses (*Tempest* 1.2.321–33):

> As wicked dew as e'er my [witch] mother brush'd,
> With raven's feather, from unwholesome fen
> Drop on you both!

Thus, for Lady Macbeth to welcome the raven's portent puts her in accord with witches' thoughts, with the Hecate of Middleton's *The Witch* (5.2.40–42):

> Raven or screech-owl never fly by the door
> But they call in, I thank 'em. And they lose not by't—
> I give 'em barley soaked in infants blood.

Lady Macbeth's castle is an "infectious house" with fatal gates to welcome Duncan.

In all these ways, Lady Macbeth certainly tries to become an intimate of evil, a communer with murdering ministers, fatal ravens, spirits who will give her suck. Does that make her a witch? Not in any technically legal or theological sense that King James (for instance) would have recognized. She does not enter into supernatural dealings with devils or their agents. There is no reciprocal activity of the sort Macbeth engages in at the necromancy. She is a witch of velleity and gestures, while he is one in fact. She forms no pact with the devil. Hecate does not appear to comfort *her*.

Notes

2. Boy actors of the requisite diction, memory, and ability to sing and dance were hard to come by in the public theater, where their very presence was under continual assault by moralists (see Chapter 2, note 7). Good boy performers had a short time to learn and perfect their skills before losing the female parts when their voices changed. Shakespeare's great termagant roles of the early 1590s, and his roles for a matched comic pair (a tall boy and a short boy) in the middle nineties, indicate how

Shakespeare tailored parts for the troupe's apprentices—as he did for its clowns, and for Burbage himself.

3. See note 28 below.

4. E.K. Chambers, *The Elizabethan Stage* (Oxford University Press, 1967), Vol. 2, p. 213.

5. One of the Merchant Taylors' men was paid thirteen shillings "for things for the boys that made the speech, viz. for garters, stockings, shoes, ribbons, and gloves." The Merchant Taylors Company's account books cited in Gerald Eades Bentley, *The Profession of Player in Shakespeare's Time, 1590–1642* (Princeton University Press, 1984), 126.

6. Compare the coaching of Moth, the "pretty knavish page," in *Love's Labour's* 5.2.98–99.

> Action and account did they teach him there.
> "Thus must thou speak," and "Thus thy body bear."

12. Mark Rose claimed that Lady Macbeth "practises witchcraft" (*Shakespearean Design*, Harvard University Press, 1972, 88). W. Moelwyn Merchant described "Lady Macbeth's willed submission to demonic power, her unequivocal resolve to lay her being open to the invasion of witchcraft" (*Aspects of Macbeth*, edited by Kenneth Muir and Philip Edwards (Cambridge University Press, 1977), 51).

13. The witches hovered near Lady Macbeth in a 1964 Austrian production of the play (Rosenberg, 201). For the same actress doubling the Lady and Hecate, see ibid., 492.

14. For ministers as angels, see Isabella's prayer at *Measure for Measure* 5.1.115: "Then, O you blessed ministers above...." See also Laertes's "A minist'ring angel shall my sister be" (*Hamlet* 5.1.248). For devils as ministers, see "minister of hell" at *1 Henry VI* 5.4.93 and *Richard III* 1.2.46, and Sycorax's "potent ministers" at *Tempest* 1.2.275. Prospero's intermediate spirits are "ministers of fate" (*Tempest* 3.3.61, 65, 87).

15. "Take" can mean "blast" or "wither," a witch-usage as at *Merry Wives* 4.4.31 (the phantom "blasts the trees and *takes* the cattle") or *Hamlet* 1.1.163–64, on the blessed Christmas time:

> then no planets strike
> No fairy *takes*, nor witch hath power to charm.

Or the verb can mean *take in exchange for*—her milk becomes the watery "gall" that ran when witches' marks were cut into. A witch named Alice Samuels had her mark cut open in 1593, and it ran "yellow with milk and water," then clear (non-white) "milk," then blood. See C. L'Estrange Ewen, *Witchcraft and Demonianism* (Heath Cranton Ltd., 1933), 173.

16. See *Newes from Scotland* (1591): "the Devil doth generally mark them with a privy mark, by reason the witches have confessed themselves that the Devil Both lick them with his tongue in some privy part of their

body before he doth receive them to be his servants" (Barbara Rosen, *Witchcraft in England: 1558–1618* (University of Massachusetts Press, 1991), 194).

17. Joan fed several devils at once, since witches often had multiple mole-teats. Margaret Wyard confessed in 1645 that "she had seven imps like flies, dors [bees], spiders, mice, and she had but five teats, and when they came to suck, they fight like pigs with a sow." C. L'Estrange Ewen, *Witch Hunting and Witch Trials* (Kegan Paul, 1929), 306. Since devils were bodiless spirits, they could appear to men only if they created phantasms of "thick air," spoke through dead human bodies, or used live animals' bodies. They could use human semen in incubus-intercourse, but they had to take it from animals' bodies to have real physical coupling. When Lady Macbeth invokes the murthering ministers' "sightless invisible] substances" at 1.5.49, she is referring to demons who have not taken familiars' animal bodies.

18. They also use their familiars to suck the life from others—the fair Rosamund was killed by toads, acting under orders from their witch. See George Lyman Kittredge, *Witchcraft in Old and New England* (Atheneum, 1972), 182–83. The conjurer-pope in Barnes's play uses serpents at the breast to kill his pederastic victims (lines 2770–89). The evil Queen Elinor in Peele's *Edward I* (lines 2094–96) kills a critic of her acts the same way.

19. Compare the "fatal raven" of *Titus* 2.3.97.

20. King John in the play is given two portents (two *adynata*) to assure him, just as Macbeth was. John will not fall until stones fight men and birds defeat armies. Then, to a deafening clamor of birds sent ahead of the French army, the earth is darkened and the English army breaks and runs, done in by "a flight of ugly ravens." Cf. *The Raigne of King Edward III*, edited by Fred Lapides (Garland Publishing, 1980). The ravens "made at noon a night unnatural / Upon the quaking and dismayed world"—like "night's predominance ... When living light should kiss [the earth] at *Macbeth* 3.4.8–9. The ravens fly in "corner'd squares," like the "brave squares of battle" at *Antony* 3.11.4 or "our squares of battle" at *Henry V* 4.2.28. For the possibility of Shakespearean authorship, see Kenneth Muir, *Shakespeare as Collaborator* (Barnes & Noble, 1960), 10–55, and Stanley Wells and Gary Taylor, *William Shakespeare: A Textual Companion* (Clarendon Press, 1987), 136–37.

21. Harpy, from Greek *harpazein*, to snatch, corresponded with the Jacobean word "gripe" for carrion birds. (This word is used for Seneca's *vultur* in the Elizabethan translations.) "Harpyr" at *I Tamburlaine* 2.7.56 is emended to "harpy" by Marlowe's editors.

22. Ben Jonson, *Works*, edited by C. H. Herford (Oxford University Press, 1941), Vol. 7, 23.

23. Ben Jonson, *The Complete Masques*, edited by Stephen Orgel (Yale University Press, 1969), 127 (lines 142–45), with Jonson's own note at 532–33.

JAN H. BLITS ON THE MEDIEVAL CHRISTIAN COSMOS

Macbeth depicts the life and soul of a Christian warrior who first becomes his kingdom's savior, then its criminal king, and finally its bloody tyrant. Set in eleventh-century Scotland, the play portrays Macbeth within the context of a moral and political order rooted in a natural order that is established by God. Far from being merely a backdrop for the play (as is often suggested), this natural order decisively shapes both the characters and the action of the drama. Shakespeare shows that what a character thinks about the natural order affects how he understands the moral and political world, and hence himself and his life. It makes him who or what he is.

The natural order that we see in *Macbeth* is a distinctly medieval Christian cosmos. Characterized by God's providence, plentitude, and pervasive presence, it appears to be a hierarchical, harmonious unity in which all being and goodness flow from God and what everything in the world is depends on God and its place in his scheme of creation. Throughout the play, something's "place" is not merely its spatial location, but its fixed "degree" or "rank" in the established order of things. Place refers to hierarchical position as well as to whereabouts in space.[1] Likewise, God is generally thought not only to see everyone's every action and to know everyone's most secret thoughts ("Heaven knows what she has known" [5.1.46]), but to protect the innocent, punish the guilty, and, indeed, to feed the birds of the air and supply their other natural needs. Nothing escapes Heaven's notice or concern. Even Macbeth and Lady Macbeth fear that Heaven will see them murdering Duncan and act to stop or to avenge the deed.[2]

Further, as God not only sees but foresees all things, and as he, moreover, does nothing directly that can be done through intermediaries, the world in *Macbeth* is pervaded by a profusion of preternatural beings with the power to prophesy and to produce magical changes or effects in things. Nature is surrounded or suffused by the supernatural. Witches, angels, devils, saints, spirits, and other such beings permeate the world and, bridging the gulf between God and the human soul, are able to see what lies ahead and to transform what human power is unable to change.[3]

Finally, since God wills and orders all things and nothing happens outside his providence, many of the characters in *Macbeth* believe that chance or fortune has little or no role in human affairs. Not only does the traditionally pious Old Man trust that good always comes of evil (2.4.40–41), but Macbeth and Lady Macbeth, on the one side, and Macduff and Lady Macduff, on the other, show by their actions as well as by their words that they believe that virtue possesses the power to govern the world. Notwithstanding their deep and direct moral opposition in other critical respects, each of them sees the world as a morally consistent order in which the virtuous are always rewarded or protected and virtue alone determines one's fate.[4]

Shakespeare leads us, however, to examine the unity, harmony, and order of this medieval Christian cosmos. The medieval world—imbued with distinct and fixed ranks, the subordination and obedience of the lower to the higher, and a strong sense of plentitude, purpose, wholeness, and order in both the temporal and the spiritual realms—may set forth the natural order in high relief.[5] But, in so doing, it also points up fundamental tensions that inhere not only within the medieval cosmos, but, by implication, within any unified, harmonious, natural order. In *Macbeth* we see two such tensions. One concerns the relation between two opposed forms of virtue; the other, the relation between virtue and life. The tensions themselves and the complex interaction between them, played out in the actions and the souls of the characters, form the essential core of the drama.

The first tension exists between the two contrasting forms of virtue esteemed in *Macbeth*'s warrior, Christian Scotland: the manly virtue practiced by men like Macbeth ("brave Macbeth (well he deserves that name)" [1.2.16]) and honored so highly by his wife, and the Christian virtue evoked by the "most sainted king" Duncan (4.3.109) and devoutly revered by Macduff. Manly virtue honors bravery, boldness, and resolution ("Be bloody, bold, and resolute" [4.1.79]); Christian virtue exalts meekness, innocence, and trust ("Whether should I fly? / I have done no harm" [4.2.72–73]).[6] The former emphasizes fear while honoring war; the latter emphasizes love while celebrating peace. Manly virtue speaks of courage, action, prowess, vengeance, and resistance. It demands action while disdaining fortune. Christian virtue speaks of pity, patience, guilt, forgiveness, and remorse. It demands innocence while trusting providence. What is fair in the light of one is foul in the light of the other.

In *Macbeth*, Christian and warrior virtue exist side by side not only in the same country, but often in the same individual.[7] While Macbeth, for example, is "Bellona's bridegroom" (1.2.55) and is spurred to Duncan's murder by his wife's accusation of unmanliness ("When you durst do it, then you were a man" [1.7.49]), he nonetheless not only looks up to Duncan's meek, angel-like virtues,[8] but, repulsed by his thoughts of murder and eventually tormented by his murderous deeds, he is finally destroyed by his own Christian conscience. Indeed, haunted by his guilty conscience, he tries to destroy it and, in so doing, ultimately destroys both his conscience and himself. If manly ambition leads Macbeth to his first crime, paradoxically it is Christian conscience that drives him to his last. Had he either listened to his Christian conscience in the beginning or never heard it at all, he would not have become a bloody tyrant in the end.

The most obvious example of these opposed virtues coexisting in the same person, each in an untempered form, is Macduff. Macduff is at once a manly warrior and a devout Christian. No one, not even Macbeth, speaks more often or more assuredly of his sword than he ("My voice is in my sword" [5.8.7]).[9] Nor does anyone else, not even the pious Old Man in act 2, scene 4, describe Scotland's moral and political events in explicitly biblical, let alone apocalyptical, terms so frequently or so emphatically as Macduff repeatedly does.[10] Macduff trusts his sword and the cross equally. Thus he flees to England to bring back an army to overthrow Macbeth ("Let us rather / Hold fast the mortal sword, and like good men / Bestride our downfall birthdom" [4.3.2–4]). But, while doing so, he leaves his wife and children undefended, trusting their protection to God. And then, upon hearing of their slaughter, he does not doubt divine providence, but blames his own sinfulness for their fate:

> Did Heaven look on,
> And would not take their part? Sinful Macduff!
> They were all struck for thee. Naught that I am,
> Not for their own demerits, but for mine,
> Fell slaughter on their souls.
> (4.3.223–27)

Even while he believes that only the mortal sword can redeem Scotland's great wrongs, Macduff also believes in the existence of a moral order in which God guarantees the victory of goodness in the world and allows only sinners (or those they love) to suffer.

Notes

1. 1.4.35–36; 1.7.61–62; 2.4.11–13; 3.1.91–102; 3.4.1–8, 118–19; 5.9.39. References are to act, scene, and line. All references to *Macbeth* are to the Arden edition, ed. Kenneth Muir (1951; reprint, London: Methuen, 1984). Where the Arden text differs from the First Folio, I have sometimes emended the quotations, based on the New Variorum Edition, ed. Horace Howard Furness Jr. (1870; reprint, New York: Dover Publications, 1966.)

2. 1.5.53–54; 1.6.3–9; 1.7.21–25; 2.3.8–11; 2.4.4–10; 4.2.30–33, 72–78; 4.3.5–8, 141–59, 223–27.

3. E.g., 1.1.5; 1.3.8–10, 48 ff.; 1.5.1–16, 29–30, 40–50; 3.1.1–10; 3.4.122–25, 131–34; 3.5.2–33; 4.1.48 ff.; 4.3.141–59; 5.3.1–10; 5.5.42–46; 5.8.8–22.

4. E.g., 1.7.59–62; 3.1.56–63; 4.2.72–73; 4.3.223–27.

5. As Sir Thomas Elyot wrote (1531), "[T]he discrepancy of degrees, whereof proceeds order, ... in things as well natural as supernatural has ever had such a preeminence, that thereby the incomprehensible majesty of God as it were by a bright learn of a torch or candle is declared to the blind inhabitants of the world." Sir Thomas Elyot, *The Boke Named the Gouernour* ed. Henry Herbert Stephen Croft, 2 vols. (London: Kegan Paul, Trench, 1883), 1:3. I have modernized the spelling.

6. For "Whether should I fly" rather than "Whither should I fly," see note 27, Act Four.

7. The close juxtaposition of the two kinds of virtue leads some critics to suggest that Christianity is still vague and only newly emerging in Macbeth's Scotland (see, e.g., H. B. Charleton, *Shakespearian Tragedy* [Cambridge: Cambridge University Press, 1971], 145ff.; Paul Cantor, *"Macbeth" und die Evangelisierung von Schottland* [Munich: Carl Friedrich von Siemens Stiftung, 1993]). However, Scotland had been converted to Christianity by St. Columba nearly half a millennium earlier. Duncan is, in fact, the last, not the first, king to be buried on "Colme-kill" (Iona) (2.4.33–35; see also 1.2.63). Note also that Malcolm's name, in Gaelic, means "Follower of St. Columba."

8. By contrast, in Holinshed's account, Shakespeare's principal source, Macbeth speaks disapprovingly, and perhaps even contemptuously, of Duncan's soft qualities. See Raphael Holinshed, *The History of Scotland*, vol. 5 of *Chronicles of England, Scotland, and Ireland* (1808; reprint, New York: AMS Press, 1965), 265. I have modernized Holinshed's spelling throughout.

9. Also 4.3.3, 87, 234; 5.7.19.

10. 2.3.62–63, 65–68, 74–79; 4.3.55–57, 108–11, 223–27, 231–35; 5.8.3,14; see also 2.4.34–35; 4.3.5–8. Macbeth comes closest, in describing his own affairs; see 1.7.16–25; 4.1.117 and 5.5.21. Macduff's moral character is largely Shakespeare's invention. Holinshed gives no hint at all of his devout Christian piety. Nor does he depict him so confident of his sword as Shakespeare does. See Holinshed, *Hist. Scot.*, 274–77.

Park Honan on Time's Perpetuity

Groups of royal swans, once the delight of Queen Elizabeth, still floated in calm indifference on the river Thames. These creatures could be seen among low, flat-bottomed barges and high-masted vessels on the smooth surface of the water. Many an actor living in the city must have stepped into a waiting, upholstered wherry and crossed within sight of the swans to Bankside—to hear news or gossip at the Rose or Globe. In the late summer of 1605 there was news of the royal patron. King James had reached Oxford on 27 August. He had been made to wait outside St John's College's gates for Matthew Gwinn's brief, pretty welcoming pageant. Three young boys, in the dress of female prophets or Sibyls, had hailed him as a descendant of the Scottish warrior Banquo. 'Nec tibi, Banquo', they told the King of England and of Scotland,

> Not to thee, Banquo! But to thy descendants
> Eternal rule was promised by immortals.

Happily not linked with the bloody usurper Macbeth, the King was next treated to Oxford's learning?[24] For two days he listened to Latin 'disputations' in theology, medicine, law, and other topics. One question debated at the college was, 'An imaginatio osit producere reales effectus?' (Whether imagination can produce actual effects?). The King's players, reaching Oxford on 9 October, may have seen the academic questions which were printed as a broadsheet. The 'imaginatio' one, by coincidence or not, is answered in *Macbeth* when the killer's imagination alone creates a dagger in the air before Duncan's murder.

Oxford's events may not have inspired Shakespeare's play, but they perhaps reminded him of Macbeth and Banquo in Holinshed's *Chronicles*. The new reign's mythology elevated Scottish history, and, by chance, regicide became a topic of talk in November in London. A horrific plan had come to light. Guido or Guy Fawkes, a Yorkshire-born soldier, had carried twenty barrels of gunpowder and many iron bars into a vault under the House of Lords with the aim of blowing up the King, the Queen, Prince Henry, the bishops, nobles, and knights, 'all at one thunderclap'.

Interestingly, Guy Fawkes was attached to a web of conspiracy which led up to the Warwickshire gentry and included Catholics known to the Shakespeares—such as Robert Catesby, whose father had held land in Stratford, Bishopton, and Shottery, and John Grant, a Snitterfield landowner. So many sympathizers and plotters were local men that a board of jurors, including July Shaw—later a witness to the dramatist's will—met at Stratford in February 1606 to investigate the Gunpowder Plot. Like Macbeth in confusing foul and fair, the plotters cannot have seemed very remote to Shakespeare. Trials and hangings meanwhile took place in London. Father Henry Garnet, the Jesuit Superior, was hanged on 3 May. His defence of the right to 'equivocate' at his trial puts one in mind of the Porter in *Macbeth* who thinks of himself at Hell's gate after Duncan is killed: 'Knock, knock.... Faith, here's an equivocator that could swear in both scales against either scale, who committed treason enough ... yet could not equivocate to heaven. O, come in, equivocator' (II. Iii. 7–11).

A few public events, then, may be traceable in *Macbeth*, but was the Scottish tragedy played for two kings in the summer of 1606? Or was it written as a 'royal play' for their sakes? In August the bristling, beflagged warship *Tre Kroner* touched Gravesend with King James's brother-in-law Christian IV of Denmark aboard. Having come over mainly to see his sister Anna, he was very well entertained. After all this was the first state visit to England by a foreign ruler in eighty-four years. A tall and almost stout, whitish-blond Dane of 29, Christian IV had an ability to drink most ordinary mortals under the table—his gentle mother is said to have worked her way 'through two gallons of Rhine wine a day'—but he had a weak grasp of his host's language. Anyway, the King's men performed three times for the two jovial monarchs. There is no hint as to which plays were staged, and no sign that *Macbeth* was one of them.[25] (Later, the tipsy shipboard scene on Pompey's yacht in *Antony and Cleopatra* is said to have recalled a shipboard feast of James and Christian, but nowhere else does the author so foolishly risk mocking his patron.)

Nevertheless *Macbeth* was sooner or later acted at James's court, and its relation to the royal patron is fascinating. In Holinshed's *Chronicles*, Shakespeare had found Banquo himself involved in a conspiracy to kill King Duncan, and this he may have changed to avoid implying that James I's ancestor was guilty of treason. Yet to have shown Macbeth and Banquo in league to murder a king would also have been faulty in dramatic terms: he clears Banquo of complicity, so that Macbeth is deprived of any excuse for killing Duncan.

At the same time he refuses to whitewash Banquo, or to give James I an ancestral paragon. Banquo in the play admits to an 'indissoluble tie' with Macbeth, and accepts the latter's accession, though fearing he played 'most foully for't'. He hopes the witches will help him, too. 'Why by the verities on thee made good', Banquo says of the Witches' aid,

> May they not be my oracles as well,
> And set me up in hope? But hush, no more.
> (III. i. 8–10)

That 'hush, no more' signifies no assault of his robust Scottish conscience, and Banquo is murdered before he can reveal other 'cursed thoughts' about his own or his descendants' prospects. Though innocent of treason he is culpable in condoning Macbeth's rule and guilty in his desire. This aspect of *Macbeth* is biographically interesting in that Shakespeare's dramatic interests, his political realism, his concern for history; psychology, and truth, are really uppermost in his mind. He does not tailor a Scottish play to suit Scottish James; he knows he must take risks, and so he takes them without being foolhardy. Later on, he apparently salutes his patron briefly in Act IV when the Witches offer a vision of Banquo's heirs (who will include James I). Macbeth in horror sees the royal line 'stretch out to th' crack of doom' (IV. I. 133). That echoes a popular notion of Shakespeare's time that James's noble line of descendants would endure to the world's end.

Otherwise *Macbeth* has rather little to do with James I, though his book *Daemonology* (1597) has remarks on witches similar to Banquo's comments. The playwright, no doubt, has read his patron's books. But Shakespeare's Witches are complex, ambiguous creatures who relate to medieval habits of mind. They undermine Macbeth. In one critic's view they become 'heroines' of the play in subverting the evil order which demonizes them,[26] but they are also mysterious and unknowable icons, images of fate, demonic tempters, and malevolent, ugly old hags with living counterparts in the 'wise women', witches, and sorcerers one might consult for a fee at London Bridge, Whitechapel, or Bankside.

Notes

24. [Matthew Gwinn], *Vertumnus sive Annus Recurrens Oxonii* ... (1607), 'Ad Regis ... tres quasi Sibyllac ...', lines 4–5.

25. Cf. H.N. Paul, *The Royal Play of Macbeth* (New York, 1978); and H. Neville Davies, 'Jacobean *Antony and Cleopatra*', *Shakespeare Studies*, 17 (1985), 123–58.

26. Terry Eagleton, *William Shakespeare* (Oxford, 1986), 2–3.

ROBERT WEIMANN ON THE SIGNIFICANCE OF THEATRICAL SPACE

On the Elizabethan stage the difference between the imaginary landscape inscribed in the story and the physical, tangible site of its production was of particular, perhaps unique, consequence. Since there was both continuity and discontinuity between these two types of space, the drama in production, drawing on both the products of the pen and the articulation of voices and bodies, could through their interactions constitute at best an 'indifferent boundary'[2] between them. In fact, the boundary between the inscribed matter and the performing agency of theatrical representations appears altogether fleeting; no matter how deep (or how deeply submerged) the cultural difference between them was, it never constituted a rigid division, let alone a binary opposition in either the semiotics or the semantics of theatrical space. Once written language was articulated orally, in the form of dramatic speech, and once performers' voices and bodies were sustained by prescribed roles, neither pen nor voice remained an isolated, univocal source of authority in the projection of theatrical space. Since this space was larger and more complex than either the writing of characters or the delivery of performers could occupy, only the given conjuncture of pen and voice could in each case decide on what grounds the place and time 'which speaks' might be larger than or otherwise different from the place and time which 'is spoken.'

The differential use of the platform stage was not of course a Shakespearean invention; it was inseparable from a division, deep in the formation and function of the Elizabethan theatre, between the cultural poetics of playing and the more distinctive literary poetics of writing. In the early modern period, bodies and texts found themselves in a new and challenging relationship involving tensions and mutually consequential engagements between two orders of socially encoded communication—the visible, audible immediacy in the articulation of speaking/hearing bodies on the one hand and, on the other, the writing, whether in manuscript or print, with its distance between production and reception, signification and interpretation.

(...)

In order to explore further the doubleness in Elizabethan projections of theatrical space, it seems helpful at this point to illustrate the Shakespearean adaptation of *locus* and *platea* conventions in a specific playtext. Focusing on the way that these double projections of space are entangled in early modern relations of authority and representation, I first propose to examine two major dramatic scenes in *Macbeth*. One—the banquet scene—is marked by an unambiguously established *locus* that is only slightly exposed to the disturbance of a *platea*-like intersection; the second—the Porter's scene—is one in which a strong residue of the *platea* is made to engage a particularly vibrant and stringently localized moment of tragic action.

The "great feast" in *Macbeth* (3.4.1–120), reaching back to earlier scenes (particularly an early banquet in the play) is, in George Hunter's words, "a climactic scene" where "bloodshed and treachery" cannot be repressed any longer (Hunter [ed.]

Macbeth 19). The scene is clearly marked by its stage properties: a table with, presumably, stools or chairs, serves to symbolize the place and occasion of a banquet in the Castle of Inverness. But the "good meeting" (3.4.108) is a vulnerable occasion, with many things at risk, in which signifying props and images are somewhat fleeting and unstable in their purpose. On this same platform stage, minutes ago, Banquo was invited to join the same festive meeting as "our chief guest" whose absence would cause "a gap in our great feast, / And all-thing unbecoming" (3.1.11–13). It was the same stage on which only two short scenes ago Macbeth, after having challenged "fate into the list" (70), i.e., into "that enclosed ground in which combats are fought" (Alexander Schmidt, *Shakespeare-Lexicon*), commissioned the murderers. Here, also, in another "swift scene" (the term is from *Henry V* [3.0.1]), but certainly applicable here), Banquo was just slain a mere four lines before the Folio's stage direction inserts "*Banquet prepar'd*," to be opened by Macbeth's "hearty welcome" (3:4:2): Even before this word of welcome is spoken, the focal point of the scene—underlined by the stage direction—is taken up by the host, who apportions the social space of privilege at the *locus* according to a given order of seating ("You know your own degrees, sit down" [3.4.1]).

The banquet scene comes at the end of this breathless sequence. The setting up of its *locus* must be assumed to have followed an established pattern, as when, in *Henry VIII*, 1.4, a similar scene was introduced by the bringing on stage of a "*table for the guests.*" The table was one on which, as early as *Cambises*, "the cloth shalbe laid" (969) and where, in *Titus Andronicus*, Titus "*like a cook*" was "placing the dishes" (5.3.25, 26). But in *Macbeth*, the "*Banquet prepar'd*" is marked by a series of "flaws and starts" (62), culminating in a situation where the host himself has "displac'd the mirth, broke the good meeting, / With most admir'd disorder" (108–09): In the process of this displacement, Macbeth himself is disordered in fulfilling his household obligations. In his own words, "You make me strange / Even to the disposition that I owe" (111–12). Having sought to "play the humble host" (4), he himself is *estranged,* emotionally as well as spatially, from both his own role and duty and his seat "I' th' midst" (10) of the occasion: The estrangement is an inward disturbance, but it is also one marked by spatial conventions informing the place and purpose of the actor's performance at the table.

The disruption sets in when the First Murderer enters with the unpublishable news that Banquo is slain and Fleance has escaped. Macbeth, leaving a physical "'gap'" in the midst of the banquet table (as if to match the one felt by Banquo's absence); intercepts the murderer and his news on a site that, largely unfocused, is semiotically distinct as well as spatially separate from the *locus* of the banquet table. Macbeth's apartness from the feasters allows for a bifold purpose of playing in that, it commingles the language of dramatic, exchange and an awareness of stage direction. Together, both sustain his elliptic, even inversionary, responses to the blood-stained murderer:

MACB. [*Goes to the door.*]
  There's blood upon thy face.
MUR.   'Tis Banquo's then.
MACB. 'Tis better thee without than he within.
                (3:4.1–14)

The resulting breach in the layout of the scene is spatial as well as social. Since the protagonist himself is the agent of rupture, a playful duplicity in his language use, the punning, topsy-turvying figure of contrariety itself, must serve to distance or transgress the *locus* convention. For a brief, transitory moment, the self-enclosed, strictly symbolic representation of the feast is broken up when the spatial order of "within" and "without" is turned upside down. At this point; Macbeth—not unlike such leading characters as Hamlet, or Prospero—uses language metadramatically, thereby underlining what Anne Righter calls the Shakespearean "equilibrium of involvement and distance" (*Shakespeare and the Idea of the Play* 205).[16] As far as Macbeth's "involvement" is at stake, the meaning is that it is better to have the blood outside, upon the murderer's face, than inside, in Banquo's veins. The chilling logic is that the blood is "without" the murderer, but it is Banquo who is without the blood.

Notes

2. Here I adopt a phrase from the title of Kirby's *Indifferent Boundaries: Spatial Concepts of Human Subjectivity*. This study reminds us that "metaphors of space," or: simply the "language of space is everywhere in theory today" and that, in particular, the concept of 'difference' when opposed to 'reference' is "a spatial concept, unimaginable or just barely imaginable outside the register of space" (1, 3). This is not the place to reassess the current critical investment in the concept of space except to acknowledge the intriguing impact of a contemporary perspective that, as in Saussure and Derrida, Kristeva and Jameson, has resulted in a sense of 'indifferent boundaries' between 'space' as a target and as a category of perception. See, in this connection, Pollock, *Vision and Difference: Femininity, Feminism, and the Histories of Art*, who attempts to view together not only "the spaces represented, or the spaces of representation, but the social spaces from which the representation is made and its reciprocal positionalities" (66).

16. On metalanguage, among others, see Pfister, "Kommentar, Metasprache und Metakommunikation in *Hamlet*."

MILLICENT BELL ON WITCHCRAFT AND PROPHECY

In Shakespeare's England, the belief that witches or sorcerers could know the future unknowable to the rest of mankind was part of their special fearsomeness. As personal futurity became more unpredictable than it had ever been, it seemed as though one could gaze into the shuttered future only with the aid of God's great enemy—such knowledge being, then, a cursed thing. The sense of menace in the ambiguous power of the necromancer who offered a forecast of events is reflected in the horror felt by Queen Elizabeth herself. Her first Parliament debated a bill to punish prophecy, and it was passed in her second Parliament. An act passed in 1581 was directed against "divers persons wickedly disposed who not only wished her majesty's death, but also by divers means practiced and sought to know how long her highness should live, and who should reign after her decease, and what changes and alterations should thereby happen." Prophecy by witchcraft was traditionally associated with plots to seize the throne. It could encourage rebellion by assuring success, or stimulate attempts at assassination by predicting the ruler's death. The Yorkshire uprising of 1549 had been blamed on the promise of success the rebels had received from "fantasticall prophecie," as Holinshed records. Predictions of an army's defeat might encourage going over to the enemy, even though it might eventually turn out that the prediction was false; Montaigne had pointed out that Francis I's lieutenant general had been so frightened by a prediction that the Emperor Charles V would defeat Francis's forces that he "revolted, and became a turn-cote on the Emperor's side, to his intolerable losse and destruction, notwithstanding all the constellations then reigning." When at the end of the play Macbeth's severed head is carried high at the end of Macduff's lance (exactly as Macbeth had carried the rebel Macdonald's head from the field of battle and placed it on Duncan's battlements before the play begins), there is a grim reminder to the audience of a traditional mockery of criminal aspiration to mount above all, an aspiration often aroused by prophecy. In the thirteenth century, a witch told the rebel Welsh chieftain Llewellyn that he would gain high place, and after his execution his mockingly crowned head was borne uplifted above the throng through London and set up on the Tower in fulfillment of just such a misleading promise of elevation as Macbeth receives. Boiled and tarred for preservation, the severed heads of the Gunpowder conspirators had been stuck up on the Bridge tower in the same mockery of their expectations.

Prophecy was felt to be not only unnatural to man but a rhetorical perversion, because it was characteristically double-dealing, like the prophecies of ancient oracles. It corresponded in its deceptive nature with the conniving subversiveness it served. But it might also be felt to be a rhetorical strategy of justified rebellion compelled to express itself in muffled language—a lie justified by its end, like the "equivocation" justified by the defendants in the Gunpowder Plot. It is not clear whether the witches' evasive prophecy to Macbeth serves some necessary end. Although his career must have had an admonitory function as Shakespeare presented it, we should also account for the impression the play sometimes gives that his criminal deeds had been historically inevitable.

We can glimpse some buried suggestion that Macbeth is the man of Machiavellian subterfuge and force appearing at a time when these attributes are called for—and that the combination can be a necessary strategy for progressive ends. The Machiavellian element in Macbeth's character can remind one of the theory of the author of *The Prince* that the stable state can be created only by calculated force and strategy that subordinates moral restraint to desirable ends. Shakespeare would have found basis for such a view of Macbeth in Holinshed. In the chronicle, a Scotland divided by civil war is actually set into order by Duncan's murderer, who governs for many peaceful years before fear of betrayal causes him to contrive the death of Banquo. Shakespeare suppresses this post facto validation of the putsch that brought Macbeth to power; he makes Macbeth's reign an explosive train of further murders and social degeneration. These are changes that erase offense to a king who might identify himself with Duncan and any would-be assassin with Macbeth—and forbid the invitation to insurrection that had been found in *Richard II*. Denied also is any specific provocation of Macbeth's defection. Shakespeare does not explain Macbeth's grievance, about which one hears only in Holinshed—that he had been entitled to election to the throne by Scottish rules and had been bypassed by Duncan's arbitrary appointment of Malcolm as his successor. In the play we are unprepared to hear him exclaim, "That is a step / On which I must fall down, or else o'erleap."

But there were always reasons for thinking that under some circumstances a strong usurper was better than a weak legitimate incumbent. In *King Lear*, as I have argued, Shakespeare had recently shown the emptiness of title without power. Holinshed's Duncan is described by the rebel warrior Macdonald as a "faint-hearted milksop, more meet to gouerne a sort of idle monks in some cloister than to haue the rule of such valiant and hardie men of warre as the Scots." Even Macbeth and Banquo, who come to the king's rescue, complained, Holinshed relates, about "the kings softnes, and ouermuch slacknesse in punishing offenders," and when they decide to plot his murder they become indistinguishable from the fierce warrior thanes who had threatened Duncan earlier. The chronicler compares Duncan with his cousin Macbeth:

> Duncane was so soft and gentle of nature, that the people wished the inclinations and maners of these two cousins to haue beene so tempered and interchangeablie bestowed betwixt them, that where the one had too muche of clemencie, and the other of crueltie, the meane vertue betwixt these two extremities might haue reigned by indifferent partition in them both.... The beginning of Duncans reigne was very quiet and peaceable, without anie notable trouble; but after it was perceiued how negligent he was in punishing offenders, manie misruled persons tooke occasion thereof to trouble the peace and quiet state of the commonwealth, by seditious commotions.

In Shakespeare's play, we know nothing about Duncan's earlier years; we simply come upon him dangerously embattled against a foreign enemy and rebels who have organized themselves against him, though the history of their enmity is denied us. To show us his character, Shakespeare allows us to see Duncan in one exquisite moment when, as he approaches Macbeth's castle, he seems responsive to the harmony of nature, generous and affectionate to his fellow-man—almost a man of a different culture from the primitive world surrounding him. His language distinguishes itself by its studied Renaissance grace:

> This castle hath a pleasant seat; the air
> Nimbly and sweetly recommends itself
> Unto our gentle senses.

Works by William Shakespeare*

Henry VI, part 1, circa 1589–1592.

Henry VI, part 2, circa 1590–1592.

Henry VI, part 3, circa 1590–1592.

Richard III, circa 1591–1592.

The Comedy of Errors, circa 1592–1594.

Venus and Adonis, 1593.

Titus Andronicus, 1594.

The Taming of the Shrew, 1594.

The Two Gentlemen of Verona, 1594.

The Rape of Lucrece, 1594.

Love's Labor's Lost, circa 1594–1595.

Sir Thomas More, circa 1594–1595.

King John, circa 1594–1596.

Richard II, circa 1595.

Romeo and Juliet, circa 1595–1596.

A Midsummer Night's Dream, circa 1595–1596.

The Merchant of Venice, circa 1596–1597.

Henry IV, part 1, circa 1596–1597.

Henry IV, part 2, circa 1597.

The Merry Wives of Windsor, 1597.

Much Ado About Nothing, circa 1598–99.

The Passionate Pilgrim, 1599.

Henry V, 1599.

Julius Caesar, 1599.

As You Like It, circa 1599–1600.

Hamlet, circa 1600–1601.

The Phoenix and the Turtle, 1601.

Twelfth Night, circa 1601–1602

Troilus and Cressida, 1601–1602.

All's Well That Ends Well, 1602–1603.

Measure for Measure, 1604.

Othello, 1604.

King Lear, 1606.

Timon of Athens, 1605–1608.

Macbeth, 1606.

Anthony and Cleopatra, 1606–1607.

Pericles, circa 1607–1608.

Coriolanus, circa 1607–1608.

Cymbeline, 1609.

Sonnets, 1609.

The Winter's Tale, 1611.

The Tempest, 1611.

Cardenio, circa 1612–1613.

Henry VIII, 1613.

The Two Noble Kinsmen, 1613.

*Dates by production

Annotated Bibliography

Bartholomeusz, Dennis. *Macbeth and the Players*. New York: Cambridge University Press, 1969.

Presents an historical examination of *Macbeth* performances from the perspective of the player who is able to provide insights into the text not available to critics and scholars. Citing the actor's unique understanding of the importance of voice, movement, gesture, and individual interpretations of a dramatic work, Bartholomeusz begins with the first performance at the Globe, and continues with a discussion of some of the greatest eighteenth, nineteenth, and twentieth century performances of *Macbeth*.

Bloom, Harold. "*Macbeth*." *Shakespeare and the Invention of the Human*. New York: Riverhead Books (1998): 516–45.

Focuses on the originality of Shakespeare's rough magic, an emblem of his enormous imaginative faculty which renders *Macbeth* "a tragedy of the imagination." Harold Bloom discusses the reasons for our inability to resist identifying with Macbeth's proleptic imagination, for he so dominates the play that we have nowhere else to turn.

Booth, Stephen. "*Macbeth*, Aristotle, Definition, and Tragedy." From "*King Lear,*" "*Macbeth,*" *Indefinition, and Tragedy*. New Haven and London: Yale University Press (1983): 81–118.

Using Aristotle's definition of tragedy as a category, *Macbeth* is described as a play in which events are delimited and the audience's experience is of a truth beyond categorical definition, a play which grants a locus for "a deed without a name."

Bradshaw, Graham. *Shakespeare's Scepticism*. New York: St. Martin's Press, 1987.

Defines Shakespeare's skepticism as a mode of thought in which "acts of valuing" are interdependent with "poetic-dramatic thinking." Given the extent to which Macbeth must deny his deepest moral needs and intense imaginative apprehensions, his first deadly act in killing Duncan is described as a catastrophic self-mutilation.

Braunmuller, A.R., ed. *Macbeth*. Cambridge and New York: Cambridge University Press, 1997.

Provides a comprehensive and scholarly introduction to *Macbeth*, discussing both legendary and historical sources, major thematic issues such as politics, temporality, superstition and language and includes an historical overview of major performances before 1800 through the modern adaptations of Kurosawa, Polanski, and Ninagawa.

Brooks, Cleanth. "The Naked Babe and the Cloak of Manliness." From *The Well Wrought Urn: Studies in the Structure of Poetry*. New York: Harcourt, Brace Jovanovich, 1975.

Using Caroline Spurgeon's identification of the "old clothes" metaphor as an expression for "an ignoble man encumbered and degraded by garments unsuited to him," Brooks expands this metaphor to symbolize the fact that Macbeth's garments are in fact stolen. His discussion focuses on the pervasive cloaking images throughout the play which underscore the theme that Macbeth can never disguise his disgraceful self.

Brown, John Russell, ed. *Focus on* Macbeth. Boston: Routledge & Kegan Paul Ltd., 1982.

A diverse collection of essays written by some very distinguished Shakespearean scholars, it includes a discussion of themes and structure, some notable historical performances as well as some essays concerned with specific historical and critical perspectives. It concludes with an afterword by John Russell Brown which discusses some of the complexities of *Macbeth*, the shortest of Shakespeare's tragedies.

———. "Macbeth." From *Shakespeare's Dramatic Style*. London: Heimemann Educational Books Ltd. (1970): 160–91.

Discusses *Macbeth* in terms of such complexities as its

interplay of allusion and ambiguity, its rapidly shifting psychological pressures, and the challenges it has presented to the most ambitious of Shakespearean actors. Brown specifically focuses on those passages which concern Macbeth alone, mostly soliloquies and simple forms of dialogue, analyzing the words, the action, and the demands they place on the actor.

Calderwood, James L. *If It Were Done:* Macbeth *and Tragic Action.* Amhearst: The University of Massachusetts Press, 1986.

Discusses *Macbeth* in three contexts: as a counter-Hamlet indebted to its predecessor play of its modes and structures of presentation; as a play in which action is both a means and object of representation, a meta-tragedy; and as a study of Shakespeare's use of violence as a dismantling of the borders between civilized and savage, good and evil.

Curry, Walter Clyde. *Shakespeare's Philosophical Patterns.* Baton Rouge: Louisiana State University Press, 1959.

Identifies *Macbeth* as a medieval Christian play within the context of a core of patrimonial doctrines transmitted from the scholastic philosophers. Curry discusses the metaphysical aspects of the weird sisters as manifestations of evil intelligences elevated by science and theology, and Macbeth's deteriorating character as a product of the inherited traditions of the Italian Renaissance, a man who suffers and in whom good is never completely destroyed.

Davidson, Clifford. *The Primrose Way: A Study of Shakespeare's Macbeth.* Conesville, Iowa: John Westburg & Associates, 1970.

Examines *Macbeth* in the context of the intellectual background of the early years of King James's reign and the role of Providence as the source of order in individual lives and history. Davidson discusses *Macbeth* within the specific historical circumstances of 1606, a time of national hysteria following the Gunpowder Plot and the fear it invoked for the life of the king.

Everett, Barbara. "*Macbeth*: Succeeding." From *Young Hamlet: Essays on Shakespeare's Tragedies*. Oxford and New York: Oxford University Press (1989): 83–105.

Discusses the shaping of *Macbeth* in terms of its presentation of a reductive human experience, a terror which produces nothing for its villian-hero. Everett examines the concept of *success*, a term through which she identifies the ambiguity of Macbeth's character, a man completely withdrawn yet violently engaged with his fellow human beings.

Goddard, Harold C. *The Meaning of Shakespeare*. Chicago: The University of Chicago Press, 1951.

Sees *Macbeth* as a study of evil through the study of murder and compares Hamlet to Macbeth as imaginative brothers, the former only thinking bloody thoughts while the latter using them as the seeds of action. Goddard maintains that, in *Macbeth*, "an undivided Hamlet" begins to spiral downward into the character of Macbeth as he exhibits Hamlet's nervous irritability and hysterical passion with his orchestration of his first crime, the murder of Duncan.

Hawkins, Michael. "History, Politics and *Macbeth*." From *Focus on* Macbeth. Boston: Routledge & Kegan Paul Ltd. (1982): 155–88.

Hawkins frames his discussion of the political issues in *Macbeth* in terms of the medieval notion of the *vita activa*, and maintains that the major characters are full participants in the active life. Hawkins attributes the brevity of the play, the rapidity of events and obsession with time as strengthening the impression of the need to seize the fleeting opportunities of the moment.

Honigmann, E.A.J. "*Macbeth*: The Murderer as Victim." *Shakespeare: Seven Tragedies: The Dramatist's Manipulation of Response*. London and Basingstoke: The Macmillan Press Ltd. (1976): 54–76.

Compares Hamlet to Brutus, both of whom he describes as intellectual heroes, finding the former to be immensely more appealing for, among other things, his sense of humor and all-embracing temperament. Honigmann maintains that with *Hamlet*, Shakespeare knew he was addressing a different audience—one which had faith in the hero's judgment. Honigmann also believes that Hamlet is peopled with "exceptionally watchful secondary characters."

Jorgensen, Paul A. *Our Naked Frailties: Sensational Art and Meaning in* Macbeth. Berkeley: University of California Press, 1971.

Focuses on the human characteristics and how it relates to fear and terror, our response to the sensational. Jorgensen examines the peculiar qualities in the language and imagery of *Macbeth*, maintaining that "the function of sensation in the play is organic in a way that it is not in any other Shakespearean tragedy."

Mack, Maynard, Jr. "The Voice in the Sword." *Killing the King: Three Studies in Shakespeare's Tragic Structure*. New Haven and London: Yale University Press, 1973.

Mack discusses the significance of the banqueting scene in *Macbeth*, an emblem which produces an elaborate imagery throughout the play and which has critical importance beyond consideration of the plot. The gregariousness and sociability of feasting serve to underscore Macbeth's murderous designs and self-imposed alienation from society and ethical obligations.

McElroy, Bernard. "*Macbeth*: The Torture of the Mind." From *Shakespeare's Mature Tragedies*. Princeton: Princeton University Press (1973): 206–37.

Discusses *Macbeth* as Shakespeare's examination of a criminal who is ambivalent about his own criminality, an almost wholly internal tragedy which dramatizes the conscience-stricken Macbeth who agonizes over his evil deeds and yet is completely committed to their realization.

Miola, Robert S. "Senecan Tyranny." From *Shakespeare the Classical Tragedy: The Influence of Seneca*. Oxford and New York: Oxford University Press (1992): 92–121.

Discusses Seneca's influence on Shakespeare and focuses on Senecan characters, language and symbolism. In his chapter, "Senecan Tyranny," Miola discusses the significance of Shakespeare's recasting of Seneca in Macbeth's statements of "monomaniacal absoluteness" and dedication to evil.

Sanders, Wilbur and Howard Jacobson. "*Macbeth*: What's Done is Done." *Shakespeare's Magnanimity: Four Tragic Heroes, Their Friends and Families*. New York: Oxford University Press (1978): 57–94.

Identifies Macbeth as an individual belonging to a pagan Scotland rather than a socialized and politicized England, where the blasted heath of the witches is similar to a Thomas Hardy landscape. Sees the world which Macbeth has inherited as one which is both "radically hostile to human nature" and utterly unalterable.

Wills, Garry. *Witches and Jesuits: Shakespeare's Macbeth*. Oxford and New York: Oxford University Press, 1995.

Beginning with a discussion of the Gunpowder Plot, Wills provides an historic overview of the constellation of factors within the play—witchcraft, equivocation, political apocalypse, tested loyalties, and secret plots.

Contributors

Harold Bloom is Sterling Professor of the Humanities at Yale University. He is the author of over 20 books, including *Shelley's Mythmaking* (1959), *The Visionary Company* (1961), *Blake's Apocalypse* (1963), *Yeats* (1970), *A Map of Misreading* (1975), *Kabbalah and Criticism* (1975), *Agon: Toward a Theory of Revisionism* (1982), *The American Religion* (1992), *The Western Canon* (1994), and *Omens of Millennium: The Gnosis of Angels, Dreams, and Resurrection* (1996). *The Anxiety of Influence* (1973) sets forth Professor Bloom's provocative theory of the literary relationships between the great writers and their predecessors. His most recent books include *Shakespeare: The Invention of the Human* (1998), a 1998 National Book Award finalist, *How to Read and Why* (2000), *Genius: A Mosaic of One Hundred Exemplary Creative Minds* (2002), and *Hamlet: Poem Unlimited* (2003). In 1999, Professor Bloom received the prestigious American Academy of Arts and Letters Gold Medal for Criticism, and in 2002 he received the Catalonia International Prize.

Janyce Marson is a doctoral student at New York University. She is writing a dissertation on the rhetoric of the mechanical in Wordsworth, Coleridge, and Mary Shelley.

Harold C. Goddard was Professor of English at Swarthmore College and the University of Chicago. He is the author of *Studies in New England Transcendentalism*, and *The Meaning of Shakespeare*.

Kenneth Muir is the author of many scholarly works, including *The Sources of Shakespeare's Plays*, *Shakespeare's Sonnets*, *Shakespeare's Comic Sequence*, and *The Singularity of Shakespeare, and Other Essays*.

A.C. Bradley was a pre-eminent Shakespearean scholar of the early 19th century. Bradley held professorships of modern literature at the University of Liverpool, of English language and literature at the University of Glasgow and of poetry at Oxford University, best known for his book *Shakespearean Tragedy*. Bradley also published *Oxford Lectures on Poetry*, which includes an essay on Shakespeare's *Antony and Cleopatra*, and *A Miscellany*, in which a well-known commentary on Tennyson's *In Memoriam* appears.

Clifford Davidson is Professor Emeritus in the Department of English at Western Michigan University. He is the author of *From Creation to Doom: The York Cycle of Mystery Plays*, and *Drama and Art: An Introduction to the Use of Evidence from the Visual Arts for the Study of Early Drama*.

E.A.J. Honigmann has been Joseph Cowen Professor of English Literature, University of Newcastle Upon Tyne. He is the author of *Myriad-Minded Shakespeare: Essays, Chiefly on the Tragedies and Problem Comedies*, 2nd ed. 1998, *The Texts of Othello and Shakespearian Revision*, and *Shakespeare: The 'Lost Years'*, 2nd ed.

John Russell Brown has been a Professor of Theatre at the University of Michigan, Ann Arbor. He is the author of many scholarly works including *Shakespeare: The Tragedies, William Shakespeare: Writing for Performance, New Sites for Shakespeare: Theatre, the Audience, and Asia*, and is the editor of numerous Shakespearean plays.

William Empson was a pre-eminent English scholar and poet and held professorships at Cambridge University and the University of Sheffield. His *Seven Types of Ambiguity*, a study of the meanings of poetry, is a classic of modern literary criticism. It was followed by *Some Versions of Pastoral* and *The Structure of Complex Words*. In *Milton's God*, Empson engaged in a vehement attack on Puritanism. His poetry *Poems* and *The Gathering Storm* were noted for its wit and metaphysical conceits. A collected edition of his poems appeared in 1955. William Empson was knighted in 1979.

Robert S. Miola is Gerard Manley Hopkins Professor of English and Lecturer in Classics at Loyola University, Baltimore, Maryland. He is the author of *Shakespeare's Rome*, *Shakespeare and Classical Comedy: The Influence of Plautus and Terence*, and *Shakespeare's Reading*.

Garry Wills has been an adjunct Professor of History at Northwestern University and has been a Professor of Classics, History and Public Policy at Johns Hopkins and Notre Dame universities. He is the author of *Saint Augustine*, *Venice, Lion City: The Religion of Empire*, *James Madison*, and *Lincoln at Gettysburg: The Words that Remade America*.

Jan H. Blits has been a Professor of Philosophy and the Politics of Education at the University of Delaware and President of the Delaware Association of Scholars. He is the author of *The Soul of Athens: Shakespeare's "A Midsummer Night's Dream,"* *Deadly Thought: Hamlet and the Human Soul*, and *The End of the Ancient Republic: Essays on Julius Caesar*.

Park Honan is Professor Emeritus of English at the School of English, University of Leeds. He is the author of several books, including *Authors' Lives: On Literary Biography and the Arts of Language*, and *Jane Austen: Her Life*.

Robert Weimann is Professor of Drama at the University of California, Irvine and a member of the Berlin-Brandenburg Academy of Arts. He is the author of several books, including *Authority and Representation in Early Modern Discourse* and *Shakespeare and the Popular Tradition in the Theater: Studies in the Social Dimension of Dramatic Form and Function*.

Millicent Bell is Professor Emerita of English at Boston University. She is the author of *Meaning in Henry James*, *Marquand: An American Life*, and the editor of several works, including *New Essays on Hawthorne's Major Tales*, and *The Cambridge Companion to Edith Wharton*.

Acknowledgments

"*Macbeth*" by Harold Goddard. From *The Meaning of Shakespeare*. Chicago: The University of Chicago Press (1951): 502–05. © 1951 by The University of Chicago Press. Reprinted by permission.

Introduction to *Macbeth* by Kenneth Muir. From *Macbeth*. London and New York: Routledge (1994): xxv–xxviii. © 1962 and 1984 by Methuen & Co. Ltd. Reprinted by permission.

"Macbeth" by A.C. Bradley. From *Shakespearean Tragedy: Lectures on Hamlet, Othello, King Lear, Macbeth*. New York: St. Martin's Press (1967): 333–36. © 1967 by St. Martin's Press. Reprinted by permission.

"The Tragedy of Macbeth" by Clifford Davidson. From *The Primrose Way: A Study of Shakespeare's* Macbeth. Conesville, Iowa: John Westburg & Associates (1970): 69–71. © 1970 by John Edward Westburg. Reprinted by permission of the publisher.

"*Macbeth*: the Murderer as Victim" by E.A.J. Honigmann. From *Shakespeare: Seven Tragedies: The Dramatist's Manipulation of Response*. London and New York: The Macmillan Press Ltd. (1976): 129–32. © 1976 by E.A.J. Honigmann. Reprinted by permission.

"Images of Death" by John Russell Brown. From *Focus on Macbeth*, edited by John Russell Brown: 8–11 © 1982 by Routledge & Keegan Paul. Reprinted by permission.

"Macbeth" by William Empson. From *Essays on Shakespeare*. Cambridge and New York: Cambridge University Press (1986): 139–41. © 1986 by William Empson. Reprinted with permission of Cambridge University Press.

Index